THE BEST OF

CORWIN

CLASSROOM MANAGEMENT

The Best of Corwin Series

Classroom Management
Jane Bluestein, Editor

Differentiated Instruction
Gayle H. Gregory, Editor

Differentiated Instruction in Literacy, Math, and Science
Leslie Laud, Editor

Educational Neuroscience
David A. Sousa, Editor

Educational Technology for School Leaders
Lynne M. Schrum, Editor

Equity
Randall B. Lindsey, Editor

Inclusive Practices
Toby J. Karten, Editor

Response to Intervention
Cara F. Shores, Editor

THE BEST OF CORWIN

CLASSROOM MANAGEMENT

JANE BLUESTEIN
Editor

With contributions by

Jane Bluestein · Renee Rosenblum-Lowden

Felicia Lowden Kimmel · David A. Sousa · Kay Burke

Donna Walker Tileston · J. Allen Queen · Bob Algozzine

Marilyn E. Gootman · Roger Pierangelo · George Giuliani

CORWIN
A SAGE Company

CORWIN
A SAGE Company

FOR INFORMATION:

Corwin
A SAGE Company
2455 Teller Road
Thousand Oaks, California 91320
(800) 233-9936
Fax: (800) 417-2466
www.corwin.com

SAGE Ltd.
1 Oliver's Yard
55 City Road
London EC1Y 1SP
United Kingdom

SAGE India Pvt. Ltd.
B 1/I 1 Mohan Cooperative
Industrial Area
Mathura Road, New Delhi 110 044
India

SAGE Asia-Pacific Pte. Ltd.
33 Pekin Street #02-01
Far East Square
Singapore 048763

Acquisitions Editor: Hudson Perigo
Associate Editor: Allison Scott
Editorial Assistant: Lisa Whitney
Production Editor: Melanie Birdsall
Typesetter: C&M Digitals (P) Ltd.
Cover Designer: Rose Storey
Graphic Designer: Nicole Franck
Permissions Editor: Adele Hutchinson

Printed in the United States of America

Library of Congress Cataloging-in-Publication Data

The best of Corwin: Classroom management/
Jane Bluestein, editor.

p. cm. — (The best of Corwin)
Includes bibliographical references and index.

ISBN 978-1-4522-1736-9 (pbk. : alk. paper)

1. Classroom management—United States.
I. Bluestein, Jane II. Corwin (Firm)

LB3011.B47 2011
371.102'4—dc23   2011034303

This book is printed on acid-free paper.

11 12 13 14 15 10 9 8 7 6 5 4 3 2 1

Contents

Preface

Jane Bluestein

Funny how things change. . . . A few years ago, I surveyed business leaders, asking them to identify the kinds of skills, attitudes, and behaviors they would like our students to bring to the workplace. I found it interesting that not one individual sought employees with the ability to "sit still and be quiet," and things like following orders or maintaining the status quo were likewise low on the list. Instead, respondents consistently emphasized critical thinking, creativity, initiative, honesty, and reliability, along with a strong work ethic and an ability to work with others. Outside-the-box thinking got a lot of votes—my favorite from a guy who interviewed prospective hires looking for qualities like "vision and attitude."

Now at this point, you may want to notice that aside from some overlap on a few of the interpersonal traits, there's a bit of a discrepancy between the qualities deemed valuable in the workforce and those deemed acceptable in our schools. (Think of how most adults in a school would respond to kids with "vision and attitude." Even critical thinking can draw fire, much less questioning authority, rules, or the point of a lesson.) Classroom management, especially in regard to inspiring cooperative and respectful student behavior, has always proved challenging for educators. However, earlier in our history, when schools, society, and the workplace were a bit more unified in their fondness for uniformity, top-down hierarchies, and fitting into assigned roles, the problems most teachers encountered paled in comparison to the range, intensity, and even danger a student's behavior can present today.

Schools have been incredibly slow to catch up with changes in our culture and economy. So many of our traditions—from the way we arrange the furniture in our room to our stubborn attachment to standardization—are throwbacks to a time when these practices supported the work environment many of our students would enter. An increasingly urgent need for change has been evident for some time. Unfortunately, most reforms rarely go beyond repackaging the same old ideas, using them in the same ways and with the same mindset as the ones they were meant to replace.

As you evaluate various approaches to classroom management (those in the following chapters or any you might run into elsewhere), ask yourself the following questions.

IS IT COMPREHENSIVE ENOUGH?

Building relationships and community is a critically important component of effective management, but so are the little details and routines. (If you've ever had a terrific lesson undone by a slight shortage of rulers, or your students' inability to use them properly, you know what I'm talking about.) Look closely at issues related to this topic, and you'll see a much bigger picture. A comprehensive approach to classroom management will inevitably address the behaviors that will prevent not only those problems sparked by unclear directions or poorly planned transitions, but also those that occur when kids compete for power, can't perform successfully on assigned tasks, lack social skills or emotional intelligence, have unmet physiological needs, or are taught in ways that make little sense to how their nervous system processes information.

Most of the programs I've seen tend to focus on a very small and generally isolated piece of this puzzle, sort of like trying to lose weight by not eating doughnuts after noon. (In itself, not a bad strategy, but generally not sufficient to achieve this goal.) In other words, behavior management isn't just about behavior. Social and emotional issues, learning styles, environmental features, teacher personality, routines and transitions, neurological and physiological needs, and academic placement and pacing will also factor in to how children behave in a classroom setting. An effective approach will account for *any* area where students might compensate for unmet needs in ways that can have a negative impact on the teacher, their classmates, the climate of the room, or their own success.

IS IT RELATIONSHIP-ORIENTED?

I understand the attraction of simple, formulaic reactions to misbehavior: It will always be easier to pull a detention slip or write a child's name on the board than it is to build relationships or, say, restructure power dynamics. Although many win-win strategies can be simple and immediately effective, the best approaches appreciate the fact that many of the processes involved in establishing positive connections with (and between) students can take time. This is especially true when you're working with kids with a history of failure, marginalization, and adversarial relationships with staff.

Connectedness positively impacts everything from attendance to academic success and correlates with a reduction in a wide range of risk factors like bullying, drug use, violence, and vandalism. Strong relationships between teachers and kids are by far the most valuable ingredient in behavior management—more effective than any rules, threat of punishment, or parent intervention. And, by the way, if you're worried about how you're going to squeeze "connecting with kids" into your already-too-full schedule, be assured that this isn't a separate curricular item or activity, but a process that will be a part of every interaction you have with your kids. Look for programs and suggestions that favor process over product, and be willing to trust any time (and mindful commitment) required to create a sense of community in your classroom.

DOES IT RESPECT *EVERYONE'S* NEEDS?

Very few adults would argue against the idea that all children need things like love, acceptance, belonging, safety, success, or limits. The one (equally basic) need people tend to forget is the one about power—that is, the desire to have some say in things that affect your life. If ever a tendency toward black-and-white thinking kicks in, it will be around this issue: "Wait a minute! If kids have power, what about teachers?" As mentioned, behavior problems can emerge if *any* of these needs are not met in positive, constructive ways. But for most of us, learning to resolve this power issue, where accommodating students' need for power doesn't disempower or disturb anyone else, is truly where the rubber meets the road.

The key here is to establish an authority relationship that allows a certain degree of freedom and autonomy for students within limits, and within the context of a safe, mutually respectful classroom environment. Even the more traditional approaches to management generally acknowledge kids' needs for power, because competition for this commodity can not only be an incredibly frustrating and toxic time waster, but also because of its potential for escalating into dangerous no-win territory. I mention this issue because of the number of programs, policies, and discipline codes I've encountered over the years that favor teacher authority to the exclusion of student autonomy. Look instead for ways to promote authority relationships that consider how *all* members of the group can get what they want.

IS IT POSITIVE?

When we're working with kids, a positive orientation will be reflected in everything from our tone of voice to the comments we make on their assignments. But positivity will show its greatest promise in the context of motivating cooperative student behavior. Shifting your focus to the positive consequences of students' behaviors from the far-more-common negative reference will change not only the energy in the power dynamics in your room, but the likelihood of your kids cooperating with you. All privileges, whether a good grade or an opportunity to work with a classmate, for example, come with a price. Stating contingencies with a positive emphasis also confers a great deal of responsibility on the kids.

Pretty much every approach to classroom management that even uses the term *consequences* does so in the context of a negative response to a negative behavior, often with a system of escalating negative consequences assigned to specific misbehaviors and indiscretions. Look for a more positive orientation. And if you're worried about bribing kids, please keep in mind that the threat of a bad grade, phone call home, time out, or detention is just as much a bribe as a chance to move on to the next book, use certain equipment, work in a center, or play in Saturday's game. There is no such thing as unmotivated behavior, and the emotional and academic costs of relying on a fear of negative outcomes will rarely be worth the small successes it may appear to buy.

DOES IT FOCUS ON PREVENTION?

It's easy to think that posting the rules and negative consequences at the beginning of school is a proactive approach to discipline and classroom management. But I'm actually talking about the strategies and intentions that change the emotional environment of the classroom in ways that will render negative student behaviors unnecessary—and unlikely. You'll know that you're working with a truly proactive approach if it focuses more on preventative teacher behaviors than on the "what do I do when . . . ?" reactions to negative student behaviors.

IS IT A GOOD MATCH FOR WHO YOU ARE?

Authenticity is one of the most powerful tools for connecting with your kids (and, indeed, with people in general). Even young kids can see something weird and discomfiting in teachers trying to be someone they're not. Some strategies and approaches will be a better fit for your values and personality than others. Look for ideas that not only make sense, but feel like who you are—or want to be.

IS IT MANAGEABLE?

I once implemented a token system, admittedly out of sheer desperation, that ended up being so complicated, unwieldy, and time consuming that I dumped the entire project in the trash. Nobody goes into education because we don't have enough stress or aggravation in our lives. Any approach that requires a tremendous amount of materials, record keeping, or things to track or remember will end up driving you around the bend. Keep it simple—and if you stick to the qualities mentioned above, it probably will be just that.

IS IT WORKING?

The bottom line for any approach you ultimately select will be its effectiveness. If you see your kids staying on task longer, working more independently, making constructive choices, treating one another respectfully, getting work done, making progress, and responding to your requests cooperatively, something is clearly working. (I say this with the obvious caveat that apparently positive results gained with antagonistic, hurtful, or draconian strategies are typically superficial, short-lived, and never worth the cost to relationships or climate.)

Take time to reflect—daily, if possible—about what's working and what you'd like to refine. Filter your choices through questions like these: Does my behavior help me connect with kids in positive ways? Does it model respectful ways to treat others? Does it protect the emotional climate of the classroom? Does it help my students connect their choices with the outcomes of their behaviors? Does it help me establish my authority without violating their needs?

If you're not happy with the approach you're using—or unsettled by what you see modeled in other teachers' behavior and may feel pressured to adopt—try something new. Look for strategies that are a good match for your belief system and personality. Make small changes gradually and trust the process, because results may be slow in coming, especially at first. Be patient with your progress and gentle with yourself when an idea doesn't work the first time.

Although I can attest to the benefits for the students, go ahead and be a little bit selfish about making these changes for your own success and sanity. Remember what brought you to this profession and imagine the joy of working with kids when you can eliminate your management headaches and actually spend your time doing what you came to do—teaching!

Introduction

Jane Bluestein

This volume is an overview of the concept of classroom management, featuring excerpts from nine works by recognized experts. The following is a synopsis of what you will find in each chapter.

Chapter 1. Managing a Win-Win Classroom

Jane Bluestein

When I was in high school, I signed up for a sculpture class. I'd taken all the prerequisites and was excited about the prospect of taking my art work into a three-dimensional realm. The teacher was new, straight out of college, and one of the coolest members of the faculty. She started the class by giving each of us a mound of clay, but no actual instructions or requirements beyond some vague request for us to express ourselves. Wow! A teacher who actually valued and encouraged our creativity! What a treat this would be—until we actually turned something in and discovered that our best efforts were only fodder for a vitriolic tirade, as she moved from project to project, ridiculing our talent, our efforts, and our masterpieces as well.

As if it hadn't been stressful enough to spend the period with no idea of what we were supposed to be doing, her response created an immediate atmosphere of anxiety and mistrust, making us all highly suspect of any chance of success (or "winning") in this program. I transferred into another class immediately. (Sadly, it would be another 30 years before I was even tempted to put my hands in clay again.) Although I learned nothing about art from this experience, I certainly gained some insights about teaching that would occur to me often throughout the course of my career.

Chapter 1 deals with some of the most basic, even mechanical, aspects of creating a win-win classroom, including strategies for reducing behavior problems that tend to occur when kids don't know what they're supposed to do or when they lack the skills (or the freedom and encouragement) to resolve problems independently and non-disruptively. Keep in mind that these ideas are only a small part of the climate and connections you create: The best instructions and preparation are not a short-cut to win-win outcomes in an otherwise hostile or antagonistic environment. Nonetheless, these are the simple, practical ingredients that, when considered, can be the difference between a great lesson with on-task, engaged students and a stressful, unproductive day for everyone concerned.

Chapter 2. They're Here

Renee Rosenblum-Lowden and Felicia Lowden Kimmel

Ah yes, that moment of truth. After a restful summer—or, more likely, one spent preparing for the coming school year—you are about to meet your students. Whether you're a veteran teacher with an established reputation or a newcomer welcoming your first group of kids, these first few interactions can set the tone for the entire year.

There's a lot to be said for first impressions. Count on the fact that your kids will be checking you out, from your leadership style and management intentions to your appearance and sense of humor. They'll want to know where you're flexible and where you draw the line. If you're good at recognize the effective middle-ground between an authoritarian and permissive power approach, you'll find a win-win role easier to assume. If you're not sure, err on the side of strictness. You can still be warm and friendly, but it's always easier to lighten up—which you'll want to do as they learn and demonstrate increasingly self-managing and responsible behaviors—than it is to rein in a group that's gone off the rails. Even if you're only a few years older than your students, they need you to be an adult.

As you run through your first-day activities, know that you are establishing a climate in which you'll be working for the next ten months or so. It's always easier when you can get off on the right foot. Connecting with kids and helping them connect with one another in positive ways will buy you goodwill that make the year a pleasure for all concerned. Chapter 2 provides some tips to help you set just the right tone on that all all-important first day.

Chapter 3. Handling Social Misbehavior

David A. Sousa

I knew I was in trouble on my first day of teaching when the first student I greeted responded to my welcome with, "I don't *do* reading." Now clearly this wasn't a personal attack: I'd just set up my classroom and nobody in the community knew who I was. OK, so I probably shouldn't have been surprised that my kids weren't anywhere nearly as excited to be there as I was, but nothing could have prepared me for the caution, defensiveness, and suspicion I encountered.

For better or worse, the brain interprets new experiences in the context of previous experiences—which, for my students, apparently weren't quite as positive or exciting as I was hoping my year with them would be. Add to that the feelings and attitudes in the community, information from parents and other adults who, over the years, had had similarly negative and contentious experiences in (and with) the school, which likewise shaped the feelings and attitudes I was seeing in my students. I knew I had a lot of work ahead trying to repair their mistrust—not just of me and the system, but of their capacity for success, achievement, and enjoyment in our classroom.

The relationship between teacher and students, and the kids' perception that their teacher is in their corner, is one of the most powerful tools at our disposal in the work we do. It is in this context that classroom climate develops, and as such, where learning happens, behavior changes, and attitudes evolve. Despite a traditional emphasis on the cognitive dimensions of education, if we ignore the social and emotional needs of our students, we do so at our peril. At every grade level, we are challenged to help our kids learn far more than what our already-overburdened curriculum guides generally include.

The good news is reflected in our capacity to help students gain social competence and fluency, and to learn skills involved in making constructive decisions and managing behaviors inspired by emotions—when we respect the need to do so, and are willing to take the time it takes to address these needs. Chapter 3 offers a neurological context for social misbehavior, as well as some brain-based intervention strategies, and provides an excellent argument in favor of connectedness in an emotionally safe learning environment.

Chapter 4. Addressing Students Who Cause Class Disruptions

Kay Burke

When Benjamin Franklin issued his famous quote about the value of an ounce of prevention, he might well have been talking about classroom management. (Actually, he was talking about fire safety, but why quibble?) Although it will always be easier to deal with problems before they actually *become* problems, it's actually far more common for most of us to go about our work just hoping the problems never happen. But problems do happen, often because kids do what they know how to do to get their needs met and, unfortunately, their compensation (or survival) strategies aren't always a great match for a positive learning environment.

Kids don't change until we change. If we want to avoid some of the challenging behaviors we encounter, it pays to frontload our efforts into building relationships and a sense of community, meeting our students' needs within the very essence and structures of our classrooms, so that they don't have to act out, disrupt, or hurt anyone to get their needs met.

Chapter 4 examines some of the reasons behind negative behaviors we see in the classroom. Perhaps the best antidote to the range of misbehaviors and bad attitudes we see, regardless of cause, comes down to how our teaching behaviors and notions about discipline establish that "ounce of prevention." For example, let's assume that all students need power (since this is generally true for all of us after our first 18 to 24 months or so). You can avoid power struggles by accommodating this need within limits or structures—which your kids also need, and which protect your authority and the safety and needs of the other students. Offering choices, soliciting student input, and recognizing their preferences in areas that affect them can make opposition and defiance seem pretty silly, if not entirely pointless.

Find ways to give all kids positive attention and recognition and watch the incidence of attention-getting disruptions decrease. And nothing topples a sense of inadequacy faster than experiencing success, whether this happens through appropriate placement and pacing, accommodating modality preferences and physiological needs, or giving students opportunities to help others. (Although it may seem counterintuitive to choose anyone but our best-behaved and highest-achieving kids for this privilege, it's the young people at the opposite end of the spectrum who reap the greatest gains in behavior, attitude, and achievement when accorded these opportunities as well.)

Anyone who has ever lost it with a student (or witnessed such an incident) knows the danger of compounding the original problem, and, in the process, compromising the emotional climate of the classroom. Finding ways to not take student behavior personally, learning to defuse potential conflict with and between kids, and focusing on student dignity as a priority will also not only model positive responses for students, but will also significantly eliminate situations that might provoke a student's desire for revenge. The point is always prevention—evident in our efforts to connect with kids, meet their needs in positive ways, and build a sense of community in our classrooms and schools—so that the quest to find and understand the causes of misbehavior will ultimately fade behind our commitment to eliminate them.

Chapter 5. Dealing With Difficult Students

Donna Walker Tileston

As a beginning teacher, I was overwhelmed by the sheer amount of information I was supposed to get through during the school year. Even if my kids were attentive and engaged (they weren't) and had all the prerequisite skills they'd need (they didn't), getting through all the content I was required to teach that year would have been a massive challenge. Fast forward from 1973, and, if anything, this situation has only gotten worse over time.

One unfortunate side effect of the information explosion in recent years is the tendency for school districts to try to cram increasing amounts of material into the curriculum. If you have any hope of getting through even a reasonable amount of this material, you'll want to focus your time on instructional pursuits rather than behavioral intervention. This means getting—and keeping—your students' attention for however long they're in your room.

There's a delicate space between students being stressed out from assignments they don't understand (or believe they can't do) and being bored out of their mind from assignments that are too easy or irrelevant. Throw in differences-in-modality preferences and an age-related attention span, and you can see the value of mixing it up enough to prevent behavior problems that occur when students are not engaged—as well as those that arise when students are taught in ways that make little sense to their nervous systems.

Chapter 5 examines a variety of factors that can impact student engagement, with strategies you can use to avoid having them drift into off-task territory. Because if ever there was a moment in teaching that will take your breath away, it will be the times you realize that your kids are so thoroughly engaged in a lesson or activity that the clean-up call or end-of-class bell comes as a disappointing surprise to them, if it even registers at all.

Chapter 6. Understanding The RCM Plan™

J. Allen Queen and Bob Algozzine

In a time when many people see cultural trends leaning increasingly in the direction of entitlement, self-absorption, and thoughtlessness, it's hard to argue with goals like building student responsibility and accountability. Despite the complexity and enormity of issues related to classroom management, most programs have these intentions at heart. So it may seem strange that the various approaches and recommendations could possibly differ as much as they do.

One of the primary complaints among beginning teachers—and the educators who work with them in the schools—centers on a lack of preparation for dealing with negative student behaviors. Indeed, forty years ago, I was getting great grades in all my teacher education classes, and although I was learning how to plan lessons, create instructional materials and displays, and develop scope and sequence charts on pretty much any topic, suggestions for dealing with student behavior were scarce. Nonetheless, information that *was* available back then was strikingly similar to the orientation of the material in Chapter 6. This was my starting point, as it is for many people in the profession, and the work I'm doing today grew out of the language, procedures, and mindset of this approach.

Sometimes ideas persist because they work, but sometimes they remain a part of the landscape simply because they're familiar. In four decades, I've seen plenty of discipline programs come and go. Nonetheless, the teachers who seemed to have the greatest success with student behavior (and the fewest problems) were the ones who were willing to step outside convention and come at this issue from a slightly different angle.

They recognize that kids with access to structure, power, success, belonging, safety, and dignity, for example, tend to behave better than kids struggling to satisfy these needs. Even shifting their emphasis from negative consequences to positive outcomes can change the power dynamics and energy in an authority relationship, building student commitment and responsibility without relying on a series of escalating negative consequences (which may have little meaning or instructional value to the student), logical and reasonable though they may be.

Get familiar with this approach, because it's a fair bet that any discipline program you encounter in your facility will have a similar orientation. This may mean support for implementing a similar program, because it will surely look like something people know, and it may mean that you can expect at least a few raised eyebrows if you try a different approach, even if you do so with great success.

Chapter 7. Harnessing and Channeling Anger Into Constructive Outlets

Marilyn E. Gootman

My first classroom was next door to another fifth-grade teacher, a woman who had been at the school forever. She was universally held up as a paragon of classroom management acumen. (At the very least, her classroom was generally far quieter than mine.) Although I soon came to see that her approach was neither a good match for my personality nor particularly useful for teaching a bunch of teacher-dependent and fearful children to develop self-management skills, I did seek her advice early on. One curious bit of counsel warned that the problems I was having existed because I failed to insist that my students "check their feelings at the door."

I had no clue where to begin and if she had the particulars, they weren't forthcoming. Subsequent inquiry into the importance of emotions to learning validated my doubts that this was even possible. In retrospect, I suspect this teacher may have actually been referring to my students' *behaviors* rather than their emotions, specifically their inability to feel their feelings (especially anger and frustration) without acting out in harmful or disruptive ways.

The alternative requires skills our kids are unlikely to learn on the street or in popular culture. It's not reasonable to ask people to disconnect from their emotions, were that even a neurological possibility. Kids come as complete packages, feelings included. Unless we're willing to settle for a classroom in which emotions seem to be the only thing happening, this means that we not only need to learn to respond effectively to the affective dimensions of the students we teach, but also to teach them ways to constructively manage their feelings themselves.

Chapter 7 offers a look at the connection between anger and the need for power and makes a strong argument in favor of these needs being met in a win-win configuration, one that recognizes the value of giving kids input and choices in things that affect them. In addition, having stumbled upon the incredible value of peer helping—an idea that started by having my students help out another teacher in the school and that eventually became the subject of my dissertation—I'm delighted to see this strategy mentioned as well. And finally, we can't talk about anger without a peek behind the curtain at our own behavior, and some of the things we can do when the stresses of the job, or life in general, trigger a strong emotional response.

Chapter 8. Avoid Win-Lose Power Strategies

Jane Bluestein

You've probably heard this one before: A young woman moves into her own apartment and asks her mom to show her how to cook. When they come to her favorite pot roast recipe, the mother instructs her daughter to set the oven, cut the vegetables, and prepare the seasoning, reminding her to cut half an inch off the end of the roast before cooking it.

"Why would I need to cut off the end?" asks the daughter.

"That's just what you do," Mom answers.

"But why?" the daughter persists.

"I do it that way because that's the way my mother taught me," she responds. "That's just the way it's done."

Weeks later, at Grandma's house, the family gets together and the daughter asks, "Grandma, tell me about the pot roast. Mom says you taught her to cut a half inch off the end before you cook it. Did you really do that?"

"Of course I did. I always cut the end off," Grandma laughed, "because that was the only way I could fit it into the pan I used."

How many of us in education use strategies in our practice simply because "that's just the way it's done"? Let's look at some common win-lose traditions, specifically those related to discipline and behavior management. Many of the ideas—which, like the pot roast recipe, have been passed down among teachers from generation to generation—have endured far beyond their usefulness, if not common sense.

Chapter 8 will challenge you to examine what you know, see, and have learned (from your experiences as a student and as a professional). Although the ideas here range from pointless and ineffective to hurtful and even dangerous, watch how hard it can be to let them go. Even if you're deeply committed to becoming a win-win teacher with a much more positive orientation to interacting with your students, the temptation to mistrust the process and turn to the familiar will continue to entice, especially on when you're tired, under stress, or having a bad day.

But we can't have it both ways. One toxic element can unravel all kinds of goodwill and good intentions. Until we are willing to look under the hood and scrutinize the components of our programs and policies, we deny ourselves the privilege of making more conscious decisions about how we act in our classrooms. And as long as we believe "that's just the way it's done," it will never dawn on us to even question the possibility of doing anything else.

Chapter 9. Understand the Behaviors of Students With Emotional and/or Behaviorial Disorders

Roger Pierangelo and George Giuliani

Kids do what works. Although adults might question the desirability of the outcomes, there is method to the apparent madness. (Negative attention is still attention, for example.) Students can be remarkably creative when it comes to meeting their needs for things like safety, dignity, belonging, success, structure, power, or worth, especially when they perceive a threat to any of these commodities. When this creativity is channeled into constructive, respectful behaviors, there's a good chance for win-win results. But many children simply react with strategies that have worked for them in the past, behaviors they have learned (or witnessed) that aren't as considerate of others' needs as they might be.

There are many stress factors in our students' lives that lie beyond our immediate control. Even in win-win classrooms, where many of the factors that minimize challenging behaviors are in place, we sometimes see these stresses erupt in disproportionately aggressive or reactive outbursts, often set off by an innocent comment or look, or even a simple schedule change. If ever you need a sharp instinct and sensitivity to a student's needs—and the energy of what's happening in your classroom—it will be when that student is getting wound up for an intense emotional reaction to something going on in the room. (This could involve the demands of an assignment, the behavior of another student, or some physiological need, for example, although even things like lighting, noises, or the weather can have an impact as well.)

There is no one-size-fits-all formula for addressing disruptive or potentially dangerous student behavior. What works with one student may not work with another, and a strategy that defused a problem yesterday can actually make things worse today. So it pays to have a pretty big bag of tricks—not only to respond to outbursts, but better still, to head them off at the pass, redirecting a student's behavior before it becomes problematic.

Although Chapter 9 focuses on kids with emotional and behavioral disorders, I believe that the material is applicable to all students. Add these strategies to the ones you use to teach students self-monitoring and self-management, and the ones that build a sense of community and cooperation in your classroom, and there's a good chance that the frequency and intensity of challenging behaviors will significantly decrease and quickly resolve.

About the Editor

A dynamic and entertaining speaker, **Dr. Jane Bluestein** has worked with thousands of educators, counselors, healthcare professionals, parents, childcare workers, and other community members worldwide. She has appeared internationally as a speaker and talk-show guest, including several appearances as a guest expert on *CNN, National Public Radio,* and *The Oprah Winfrey Show.*

Dr. Bluestein specializes in programs and resources geared to provide practical and meaningful information, training, and hope in areas related to relationship building, effective instruction and guidance, and personal development. Much of her work focuses on interactions between adults and children, especially children at risk. Her down-to-earth speaking style, practicality, sense of humor, and numerous stories and examples make her ideas clear and accessible to her audiences.

Dr. Bluestein is an award-winning author whose books include *Creating Emotionally Safe Schools; High School's Not Forever; 21st Century Discipline; Being a Successful Teacher; Parents, Teens, and Boundaries; The Parent's Little Book of Lists: Do's and Don'ts of Effective Parenting; Mentors, Masters, and Mrs. McGregor: Stories of Teachers Making a Difference;* and *Magic, Miracles & Synchronicity: A Journal of Gratitude and Awareness.* Dr. Bluestein's latest books include *The Win-Win Classroom* and a companion facilitator's guide.

Formerly a classroom teacher in inner-city Pittsburgh, Pennsylvania, crisis-intervention counselor, teacher training program coordinator, and volunteer with high-risk teens at a local day treatment program, Dr. Bluestein currently heads Instructional Support Services, Inc., a consulting and resource firm in Albuquerque, New Mexico.

Her words will touch your heart; her ideas will change your life.

About the Contributors

Bob Algozzine is a professor in the Department of Educational Leadership at the University of North Carolina, Charlotte, and project codirector of the U.S. Department of Education-Supported Behavior and Reading Improvement Center. With twenty-five years of research experience and extensive, firsthand knowledge of teaching students classified as seriously emotionally disturbed, he is a uniquely qualified staff developer, conference speaker, and teacher of behavior management and effective teaching. He is active in special education practice as a partner and collaborator with professionals in the Charlotte-Mecklenburg schools in North Carolina and as an editor of several journals focused on special education. He has written more than 250 manuscripts on special education topics, including many books and textbooks on how to manage emotional- and social-behavior problems.

Kay Burke, PhD, is an author and international consultant who presents practical and interactive professional development workshops to motivate administrators and teachers. She has served as a classroom teacher, department chairperson, dean of students, assistant principal, university instructor, director of a master's degree program, and senior vice-president of a publishing company. Her doctorate from Georgia State University in Atlanta focused on helping students improve their performance on standardized tests. She has received numerous teaching awards including DeKalb County's Teacher of the Year, semifinalist for Georgia Teacher of the Year, STAR Teacher for Georgia, Distinguished Georgia Educator, and a Certificate of Excellence from President Ronald Reagan.

For the past nineteen years, Dr. Burke has facilitated professional development workshops that help educators embed standards into their instruction and improve student achievement by demanding rigor and relevance in their formative and summative assessments. She has presented at conferences sponsored by the Association for Supervision and Curriculum Development (ASCD), National Staff Development Council (NSDC), the National Association of Elementary School Principals (NAESP), the National Association of Secondary School Principals (NASSP), the National Middle School Association (NMSA), the International Reading Association (IRA), and international conferences in Australia and Canada.

Dr. Burke has written or edited fifteen books in the areas of standards-based learning, formative assessment, balanced assessment, classroom management, mentoring, and portfolios. She is a coauthor of *Foundations of Meaningful Educational Assessment* (2009) and the coauthor of *The Portfolio Connection: Student Work Linked to Standards*, 3rd ed. (2008). Some of her other books published by Corwin include *What to Do With the Kid Who . . . : Developing Cooperation, Self-Discipline and Responsibility in the Classroom*, 3rd ed. (2008); *Facilitator's Guide for What to Do With the Kid Who . . . : Developing Cooperation, Self-Discipline, and Responsibility in the Classroom* (2009); and her best-selling book *From Standards to Rubrics in Six Steps: Tools for Assessing Student Learning, K–8*, which was named a 2007 finalist for the Distinguished Achievement Award from the Association of Educational Publishers. She may be contacted through the Kay Burke & Associates' website at www.kayburke.com, by e-mail at kay@kayburke.com, or by calling (706) 319-7609.

Dr. George Giuliani, JD, PsyD, is a full-time tenured associate professor and the director of Special Education at Hofstra University's School of Education and Allied Human Services in the Department of Counseling, Research, Special Education, and Rehabilitation. Dr. Giuliani earned his BA from the College of the Holy Cross, MS from St. John's University, JD from City University Law School, and PsyD from Rutgers University, the Graduate School of Applied and Professional Psychology. He earned Board Certification as a Diplomate Fellow in Student and Adolescent Psychology and Forensic Psychology from the International College of Professional Psychology. Dr. Giuliani is also a New York State–licensed psychologist and certified school psychologist and has an extensive private practice focusing on students with special needs. He is a member of the American Psychological Association, New York State Psychological Association, National Association of School Psychologists, Suffolk County Psychological Association, Psi Chi, American Association of University Professors, and the Council for Exceptional Students.

Dr. Giuliani is the president of the National Association of Parents with Children in Special Education (NAPCSE), executive director of the National Association of Special Education Teachers (NASET), and executive director of the American Academy of Special Education Professionals (AASEP). He is a consultant for school districts and early childhood agencies and has provided numerous workshops for parents and guardians and teachers on a variety of special education and psychological topics. Dr. Giuliani is the coauthor of numerous books by Corwin, including *The Big Book of Special Education Resources* and the *Step-by-Step Guide for Educators* series.

Marilyn E. Gootman, EdD, is founder of Gootman Education Associates, an educational consulting company that provides workshops and seminars for parents and educators that focus on successful strategies for raising and teaching children. She has been in the teaching profession for more than 25 years, and her teaching experiences range from elementary school to the university level. She holds degrees from Simmons College and Brandeis University and a doctorate from the University of Georgia. Dr. Gootman has authored two books reflecting her vision that adults can guide children to become successful learners and responsible, productive citizens: *The Caring Teacher's Guide to Discipline* and *The Loving Parents' Guide to Discipline.* She is also concerned with helping children and teenagers cope with life's difficult circumstances. She wrote *When a Friend Dies: A Book for Teens About Grieving and Healing,* a book that speaks reassuringly to teens to help them through such an ordeal. Her media appearances include CNN and other major networks as well as radio and television broadcasts throughout the United States and Canada.

Felicia Lowden Kimmel grew up in Brooklyn, New York. She began her career in education as a high school English to Speakers of Other Languages (ESOL) and English teacher in San Francisco before returning east to teach in the Washington, D.C. area. She was selected to lead a Peer Mediation program at Annandale High School in Fairfax County, Virginia. Her program received a great deal of attention and received national praise after the tragedy at Columbine. She was spot-lighted as a panelist for NPR's "All Things Considered" and was a featured guest on WPGC's "Stop the Violence." After several years in this capacity, she joined the high school's guidance department while still continuing her involvement in conflict resolution. Ms. Lowden Kimmel has also worked with school districts' faculties on understanding prejudice.

Currently, Ms. Lowden Kimmel is working as a school counselor in Montgomery County, Maryland. She lives in Olney with her husband, Troy, their two daughters, Isabella and Lexi, and their dog, Maggie.

Dr. Roger Pierangelo, PhD, is an associate professor in the Department of Special Education and Literacy at Long Island University. He has been an administrator of special education programs; served for 18 years as a permanent member of Committees on Special Education; has over 30 years of experience in the public school system as a general education classroom teacher and school psychologist; and serves as a consultant to numerous private and public schools, PTA, and SEPTA groups. Dr. Pierangelo has also been an evaluator for the New York State Office of Vocational and Rehabilitative Services and a director of a private clinic. He is a New York State–licensed clinical psychologist, a certified school psychologist, and a Board Certified Diplomate Fellow in Student and Adolescent Psychology and Forensic Psychology. Dr. Pierangelo is the executive director of the National Association of Special Education Teachers (NASET) and an executive director of the American Academy of Special Education Professionals (AASEP). He also holds the office of vice president of the National Association of Parents with Children in Special Education (NAPCSE).

Dr. Pierangelo earned his BS from St. John's University, MS from Queens College, Professional Diploma from Queens College, PhD from Yeshiva University, and Diplomate Fellow in Student and Adolescent Psychology and Forensic Psychology from the International College of Professional Psychology. Dr. Pierangelo is a member of the American Psychological Association, New York State Psychological Association, Nassau County Psychological Association, New York State Union of Teachers, and Phi Delta Kappa.

Dr. Pierangelo is the author of multiple books by Corwin, including *The Big Book of Special Education Resources* and the *Step-by-Step Guide for Educators* series.

J. Allen Queen is a professor of educational leadership and former chair of the Department of Educational Leadership at the University of North Carolina, Charlotte. As a former classroom teacher, principal, college administrator, and university instructor, he has consulted in almost five hundred schools and districts, in forty-eight states and five foreign countries. He covers all areas of effective school discipline and responsible classroom management, and in addition, his work includes school violence and safe schools, successful student transitions, and drop-out prevention. He has written over fifty books and one hundred articles, including books for children on karate, in which he holds the rank of fifth degree black belt. He attributes his own sense of responsibility, civility, and respect, along with gains in self-confidence, to this martial art and popular sport. He has appeared on numerous radio and television programs, including *ABC World News,* where he was invited to discuss the problems that negative student transitions and ineffective classroom-management procedures have on school attendance and drop-out rates.

Renee Rosenblum-Lowden has taught children and adolescents for more than 25 years in the New York City school system. Currently, she is sharing her love for teaching by presenting seminars and keynote speeches to new and veteran teachers throughout the country, as well as to student teachers at various universities. She uses a sense of humor while arming them with great strategies for making classrooms safe and fun—while always being in control. She has developed a curriculum called Prejudice Awareness, using consciousness-raising techniques and incorporating her training in conflict resolution. She was selected by the NYC Board of Education to train teachers in this subject.

Ms. Rosenblum-Lowden has conducted workshops for improving communication with children and adolescents, using non-confrontational strategies for parents and teachers. Having taught family living and sex education classes, she has unique insights into the needs of her students. Ms. Rosenblum-Lowden did her undergraduate work at Long Island University and studied at The New School for Social Research and New York University. She continues to be a social activist. She is a transplanted

New Yorker who is now living in Columbia, Maryland, with her husband, Michael, and their dog, Susie B. Anthony.

David A. Sousa, EdD, an international consultant in educational neuroscience, has conducted workshops in hundreds of school districts on brain research and science education at the pre-K to Grade 12 and university levels. He frequently presents at national conventions of educational organizations and to regional and local school districts across the United States, Canada, Europe, Australia, New Zealand, and Asia. Dr. Sousa has a bachelor of science degree in chemistry from Bridgewater (Massachusetts) State University, a master of arts degree in teaching science from Harvard University, and a doctorate from Rutgers University. His teaching experience covers all levels. He has taught high school science and has served as a K–12 director of science, a supervisor of instruction, and a district superintendent in New Jersey schools. He has been an adjunct professor of education at Seton Hall University and a visiting lecturer at Rutgers University. A past president of the National Staff Development Council, Dr. Sousa has edited science books and published numerous articles in leading educational journals on staff development, science education, and brain research. He has received awards from professional associations, school districts, and Bridgewater State University (Distinguished Alumni Award), and several honorary doctorates for his commitment and contributions to research, staff development, and science education. He has been interviewed on the NBC *Today* show and on National Public Radio about his work with schools using brain research.

Donna Walker Tileston is a veteran teacher of three decades, a best-selling and award-winning author, and a full-time consultant. She is the president of Strategic Teaching & Learning, which provides services to schools throughout the United States, Canada, and worldwide. She is the author of more than 20 books, including *What Every Teacher Should Know: The 10-Book Collection* (Corwin, 2004), which won the Association of Educational Publishers' 2004 Distinguished Achievement Award as a Professional Development Handbook. She has also written the following for Corwin: *Closing the Poverty and Culture Gap: Strategies to Reach Every Student* (2009); *Teaching Strategies That Prepare Students for High-Stakes Tests* (2008); *Teaching Strategies for Active Learning: Five Essentials for Your Teaching Plan* (2007); *What Every Parent Should Know About Schools, Standards, and High-Stakes Tests* (2006); *Ten Best Teaching Practices: How Brain Research, Learning Styles, and Standards Define Teaching Competencies, Second Edition* (2005); *Training Manual for What Every Teacher Should Know* (2005); *What Every Teacher Should Know About Learning, Memory, and the Brain* (2004); *What Every Teacher Should Know About Diverse Learners* (2004); *What Every Teacher Should Know About Instructional Planning* (2004); *What Every Teacher Should Know About Effective Teaching Strategies* (2004) ; *What Every Teacher Should Know About Classroom Management and Discipline* (2004); *What Every Teacher*

Should Know About Student Assessment (2004); *What Every Teacher Should Know About Special Learners* (2004); *What Every Teacher Should Know About Media and Technology* (2004); *What Every Teacher Should Know About the Profession and Politics of Teaching* (2004); *What Every Teacher Should Know: The 10-Book Collection* (2004); and *Strategies for Teaching Differently: On the Block or Not* (1998).

She received her bachelor's degree from The University of North Texas, her master's from East Texas State University, and her doctorate from Texas A&M University, Commerce. She may be reached at www .wetsk.com.

1

Managing a Win-Win Classroom

Jane Bluestein

A few weeks into my first year, I presented my students with what I believed to be a perfect lesson. I had designed a well-orchestrated environment with elaborate plans, plenty of materials to go around, color-coded direction cards, and enough stimulating activities to keep them all busy until Easter. These kids were in fifth grade, some practically in their teens; certainly they would be able to navigate the work centers under my watchful, nurturing, facilitating care. Right?

Wrong.

For starters, no one at the mural center could agree on a theme. The kids in the media corner were fighting over who would operate the projector. And all the markers for the art activity mysteriously vanished within the first minute of class. Evidently no one had ever worked with a ruler or used an encyclopedia before, and although I had explained everything inside and out, I had a steady stream of kids tugging on my sleeve asking me what they were supposed to do. I stood in amazement, watching weeks of planning and work go straight down the tubes. In the midst of the chaos, all I could think was, "But I laminated everything!"

I received two shocks that day. I had expected my creativity to carry far more weight than it actually did; instead, it was unappreciated and overwhelming. Second, I had expected the students, who seemed so mature and streetwise, to have already acquired cer-

> It seemed as if my expectations were actually *creating* problems. Now what?

tain responsible learning behaviors. Yet they were unable to work independently in small groups, care for materials, or make decisions about their learning. It seemed as if my expectations were actually *creating* problems. Now what?

WHAT'S WRONG WITH EXPECTATIONS?

Most of us enter the teaching profession with all sorts of expectations—conscious and unconscious. Depending on what we believe our students can (or should) do, what we hear from other teachers, and our values and sense of our own capabilities, we construct a mental picture of a classroom that may or may not reflect the reality we encounter.

To make things more interesting, how often have we heard that children perform to the level of expectations and that teachers with high expectations end up with students who perform better than teachers with low expectations? Given this admonition, I introduced myself to my first class with a long list of my expectations: "I expect you to take care of materials" "I expect you to behave respectfully," "I expect you to put your names on your papers," "I expect you to love learning," and so on. Imagine my consternation when the students countered my pronouncements with bored looks, eyes rolled to the ceiling, and an exasperated chorus, after a few seconds' silence: "So?" This is where I first discovered that all too often, "high expectations" is a metaphor for wishful thinking. Clearly, the only person committed to my expectations was me!

> Clearly, the only person committed to my expectations was me!

Maybe teachers with high expectations do get better results, but this experience led me to suspect that these individuals have more going for them than their expectations, and I strongly doubt that it is the expectations themselves that generate high performance. I imagine that the students' performance is more likely to be a reflection of intention, inspired by the teacher's beliefs and behaviors, than by his or her expectations. True, we won't get much out of kids we don't ultimately believe in, but believing that students can learn, achieve, or cooperate—and teaching to their capabilities and potential—is quite different from simply expecting them to perform.

One of the problems with having expectations is the lack of commitment from the person or people on whom we project our expectations. Simply expecting does not secure agreement or generate commitment to learning or cooperation, certainly not as effectively as win-win power dynamics, interactions, and relationships or opportunities to experience fun, success, belonging, discovery, or power, for example. Additionally, our expressed expectations are often at odds with our faith in our students; kids can have a pretty sharp instinct for adults who don't believe in them.

It's also easier to have an expectation than it is to actually ask for what we want—a behavior that is often discouraged in our culture despite the fact that in the absence of this skill, we often resort to far more toxic alternatives like powering, manipulation, passive-aggressiveness, or constantly being disappointed by not getting our needs met. Perhaps we can use our expectations as a means of identifying our intentions and what we would like from others. In this sense, expectations are simply starting points, great places from which to anticipate what we want to accomplish and what we'll need (or need to do) to achieve our goals. Nonetheless, I'm betting we'll get a lot farther with things like clear limits, positive incentives, encouragement, direct requests, and a belief in our students' ability to learn and grow, than with even the most reasonable and well-stated expectations.

TURNING EXPECTATIONS INTO INSTRUCTIONS

While I was wrestling with this issue of expectations, my students were visiting Mr. Grey for art twice a week. When they came back from his class, I would ask them what they had done. Each report detailed monotonous exercises such as getting the scissors out of a box, putting the lid back on the box, putting the box back in the cabinet, sitting down with the scissors, then putting the scissors back again, and so on, over and over. For the first few days of school, the kids did nothing besides practice getting, holding, passing, using, and returning the things they'd need for art class. Period.

I asked Mr. Grey what he was up to. "Don't you have a curriculum to get through this year?"

"I sure do, and it's massive," he replied. "But if we don't do this first, we'll never get through any of it."

"You mean to tell me that these kids don't know how to get paint jars out of a storage closet?"

"Some do, sure. But most don't. Or at least they don't think about it on their own. This way, there are no questions later about where things go or how I expect them to be used."

There was that word again. "Don't you expect them to know this stuff?"

"It doesn't matter. I can expect all day long and never get what I want. Expecting kids to clean calligraphy pens and put them back in the boxes doesn't teach them how to do it. I still have to show them."

It was true. Few teachers placed higher demands on the kids than Mr. Grey. But it was neither these demands nor Mr. Grey's expectations that turned his classroom into an exciting and productive place. While he may have started with a mental picture of busy, capable, independent, and responsible students—and a great deal of faith in their ability to rise to the challenges he'd present to them—he did not leave their behavior to chance or forge ahead on a set of assumptions about what these kids should know. If Mr. Grey expected success from his students, he certainly gave them the training necessary to fulfill his objectives.[1]

YOU WANT ME TO DO *WHAT?*

Sometimes, little misunderstandings can turn into bigger problems. When success is elusive, whether because of unclear directions, lack of prerequisite skills, or absence of self-management capabilities, chaos and discipline problems are sure to follow. I was observing a new teacher during the first day of school as she announced to her kindergarten class that it was time to get in line. A few students stopped and stared; the others started running around the room. In the mayhem, I wondered if "Get in Line" was some strange new game until one five year-old came up and asked the teacher, "What's a line?"

We know that our students need clear instructions to succeed at the tasks we set before them, but what could be more clear than "Get in line"? As that new teacher quickly found out, instructions are clear only if the students understand them. The request to "Get in line" assumes that they know what a line is, where it starts and ends, which way to face, whether it is single- or double-file, and all

> Instructions are clear only if the students understand them.

other conditions regarding talking, touching, and what, if anything, they need to take with them when they get in line. She may as well have given the directions in another language. Imagine the confusion possible with more complex assignments.

Lack of clarity is a common problem in giving directions. For the student, not knowing what to do becomes a source of confusion, helplessness, frustration, and feelings of inadequacy. (I once saw an entire class of first graders break down in tears when the teacher innocently announced that they could go home as soon as they "pick up the floor." Another teacher told me that she could barely get her kids to come in out of the rain and mud after telling them they had to "scrape off their feet" first.) Poorly communicated instructions also build teacher dependence, waste time, and often result in reactive or negative feedback from teachers. We can avoid these pitfalls by getting very clear, in our own minds, about what we want, and then breaking down the directions step by step and using language the students are not likely to misconstrue, especially the first time we ask them to do something. It can also help to walk the students through each step of the directions, particularly those involved with routines, the use of equipment or materials, or movement, to increase the likelihood of their success. Remember, if it's important to us, it's worth the time to think through our goals, state our instructions in ways that reduce ambiguity and vagueness, and increase the odds of our kids' success with however much practice they need.

INCREASING SUCCESS

When one of my eighth graders interpreted my instructions to "behave yourself in the media center" to mean that he shouldn't smoke in there, it dawned on me that sometimes our kids create very different pictures in their minds from the directions they receive than the images we try to convey with our instructions or requests. To promote clarity, let's be careful about the adjectives we use. We know what we mean by *good* handwriting, *exciting* characters, *thorough* research, and *clear* presentation. Do they? Do we let them know, before their work ends up on our desks, the particular skills we will evaluate? Telling them what we're looking for, or grading for, helps focus students' efforts and promote success.

> To promote clarity, let's be careful about the adjectives we use.

Students are bombarded with verbal instructions from teachers and other adults, as well as written instructions from books, the board, and assignments. It's no wonder that they often tune us out. But even when they are focused and engaged, we don't always give directions in a way that makes sense to their nervous systems. We will almost always have a wide variety of learning styles among the students in our classes or groups, and providing instructions in more than one way can help ensure wider success, even with the simplest instructions. This is especially true when introducing more complex tasks or new routines.

For example, instructing a group to do "the first ten problems on Page 86 and any five problems on Page 93" might be fine for our auditory learners (if they are really listening), but other students will have greater success with some additional cues. Writing the directions on the board, in a folder, or on a task card can serve as a reminder and a learning aid for these students. Written instructions also free us to move on to other tasks. Once we've given our instructions in oral and written form, the students have recourse to something besides bothering the teacher with questions about "what page?" or "which problems?" When possible, using codes (like colors or symbols), cues, or illustrations with written directions encourages independence, even among poor readers or very young students. If sequence is important, listing the steps in a specific order is essential, particularly with projects that involve a number of steps; writing and numbering the directions also helps.

We can also make success-oriented decisions about when to give instructions. I've seen far too many lessons fail—and far too much time wasted when teachers have to repeat directions over and over—because the teacher did not have the students' attention when directions were given.[2] Sometimes waiting a few seconds until they finish putting things away or get settled in their seats or the work area will save time and prevent confusion down the road. If we give information to students without first asking for their attention, we shouldn't be too surprised when the majority get it wrong.

Say It Once!

Here are tips to ensure that you never have to repeat your instructions:

- Be sure you have the students' attention first. Wait until they have finished talking, writing, or cleaning up, for example, before you begin speaking. Use an auditory signal (e.g., bell, chime, a phrase or word like "Look at me" or "Freeze") to help shift their attention.
- Give the instructions verbally, as simply and clearly as possible.
- Make sure the instructions are available in written form as well, on the board or on their papers (or on a task card, for example).
- Make it okay for kids to ask one another for clarification. (If you have many kids asking each other for help, you may want to back up and reexplain what you want to the entire class or group.)
- Let the parents know your policy for giving directions before you implement it and the options their children will have, just in case a story gets home that claims "the teacher wouldn't tell me what to do."

If you need to interrupt their work, a signal from a bell or chimes, flashing lights, or clapping hands, for example, creates a shift in the auditory or visual field and can be very effective at getting your students' attention. Giving directions to inattentive students communicates a lack of self-respect (you are worth listening to, aren't you?), and it sets them up to fail as well. Likewise, hold off, if possible, on presenting new or important instructions as kids are getting ready for lunch or dismissal if the information can wait; unless those instructions have fairly immediate relevance, they'll probably be remembered better at another time.

> Good instructions offer structure.

In addition to clarity, good instructions offer structure. "Choices within limits"—the anthem of the win-win classroom—applies quite clearly to the directions we give. But if the limits are too broad, students can be overwhelmed. Although some kids can turn the vaguest instructions into creative and meaningful learning experiences, others, regardless of age, need a starting point—something concrete from which to depart. These students will find a certain amount of security, for example, in writing from a story starter or turning a simple design into a drawing. This initial structure makes it easier for them to eventually face a blank piece of paper than starting from scratch. We can also provide structure by limiting length (one

> Although some kids can turn the vaguest instructions into creative and meaningful learning experiences, others, regardless of age, need a starting point—something concrete from which to depart.

side of a paper), media (a picture made on the computer), expression (written in the present tense, drawn with only one color of ink), content (using all twenty spelling words, people involved in the women's movement during the 1970s), or any number of criteria.

Our ultimate objectives for any assignment will help us determine which choices we can offer and the amount of structure necessary. Many teachers now use rubrics with levels of completion or competence according to a list of the important components and criteria of the work assigned. This information gives a clear description of what the students need to do to attain the score at each level.[3]

Educator Jo Ann Freiberg insists that "learning should not have to be a secret! Helping students be successful means providing them with helpful and structured guidance." She notes, for example, that students study harder for an exam when they have a study guide than when they are just told to "study everything we've been over so far." Regardless of how the information is presented, identifying details about tasks to be done or specifying the criteria for a particular assignment can save a great amount of time in reexplaining and help avoid student confusion and mistakes as well.[4]

GIVE THEM A GOOD REASON

As we saw in the value of stating our boundaries positively, the language we choose in giving directions can help us encourage cooperation, build responsibility, avoid reinforcing teacher dependence, and discourage rebelliousness. Since our language and attitude are so closely linked, changing one will invariably change the other. As we commit to a positive, win-win focus, we will become increasingly aware of negative tendencies in our words and the tone of our voice. Likewise, as we shift from threats and warnings to promises and positively stated contingencies, our attitude mirrors that change.

Similarly, the reasons we give for asking for certain behaviors can either work for or against us. Our instructions and boundaries are most effective when they appear to make sense to our students. In power-based, authority relationships, the reason for doing something, whether stated or not, is connected to the power of the authority and the punitive consequences of noncompliance. Asking students to "do it for me" may not sound particularly authoritarian, but the implication of conditional approval actually works in the same manner as "do it or else."

In a win-win classroom, teachers give kids credit for being able to make positive choices even when the outcomes do not involve the threat of deprivation or punitive consequences. "Please put the lids back on the paint jars so the paint doesn't dry out" communicates much more respect for students than "Put the lids back on these paint jars or you'll never see them again." There is a clear and sensible reason for putting the lids on the jars; the request has nothing to do with the teacher's power and in no way threatens to compromise the emotional climate in the classroom.

When we ask our students to do something, we usually have a better reason for asking them than "because I said so." The actual, logical, and intrinsic reason for a boundary—so the markers don't dry out, so that we don't disturb anyone on our way down the hall, so that no one trips and falls, so that we'll have time to hear the entire story—can help build commitment and cooperation, and engage otherwise defensive or defiant students in ways that simple commands never will. These criteria are stated for the benefit of the student and the class as a whole. The request has nothing to do with the teacher's needs—although, as part of the group, these needs will be served as well. The fact that this approach clearly focuses on what's in it for the students, individually or as a group, can account for an increase in cooperation. It may take a few extra seconds, but the extra information we provide in giving the students a practical reason for doing what we ask fosters respect for the value of the task and for our request as well.

> It was certainly easier to get irritated and blame parents or previous teachers who either never had bothered to teach these skills to my students, or whose instructions, for whatever reason, just didn't seem to transfer to my room.

All of these techniques will work best when we can overcome the resistance to having to explain our requests, especially when it comes to things we believe students should already know in the first place. For a long time, I honestly resented having to take time to show fifth graders how to correctly use the pencil sharpener, to show eighth grade gang members how to put books back on a shelf, or to end each of seven classes with a daily reminder to push the chairs under the desks. It was certainly easier to get irritated and blame parents or previous teachers who either never had bothered to teach these skills to my students, or whose instructions, for whatever reason, just didn't seem to transfer to my room.

And yet, when I finally surrendered to these necessities, a few things happened, not the least of which was that my life in school got easier and my relationships—with my students and my job—improved. The few minutes I devoted to these seemingly redundant instructions and my eventual willingness to repeat them ad nauseam significantly increased the likelihood that I would get what I wanted. Better still, after a few weeks, the end-of-class bell would consistently elicit a chorus of kids, mockingly reminding everyone to "push in your chairs."

To be honest, I'm not sure I even had a logical reason for wanting the chairs pushed in. If I were really reaching, I suppose I could argue for safety's sake—a common justification despite the fact that the chairs didn't really pose much of a threat. I think I was just after whatever reduction in chaos a room full of pushed-in chairs might represent. Maybe it was just a "thing" I had, but the fact that the kids were willing to humor my fixation and accept my priorities and quirks was ultimately far more valuable to me than anything they might have done with the furniture.

USING EXPECTATIONS CONSTRUCTIVELY

It can be disappointing to discover that entering an inspiring classroom environment does not trigger some magic that enables children to use a pencil sharpener, recap the paste, alphabetize resource books, or move around the room nondisruptively. Even if the lessons are well planned and our mood is positive and enthusiastic, without information, instruction, and guided practice, we actually doom our students—and ourselves—to failure.

There are hidden assumptions and expectations in every lesson we plan. We will do well to take nothing for granted. Even if we firmly believe that they should know how to handle science equipment, use a dictionary, work with a partner, move to various parts of the room, staple papers together, or put their assignments in a particular place, it's possible that at least a few will not. Certain routines and procedures may be so basic or obvious that they're easy to overlook, especially for teachers new to the profession or those working with a grade level in which they haven't had much experience. Obviously, we cannot predict every single need that will arise, but the better we can account for the skills and behaviors our activities demand, the better we can plan for success, and the less likely we are to be undermined by students' confusion, frustration, or ineptness.

We will often need to invest time in filling the gap between where the students are and where we would like them to be. I once had a group of high-risk eighth graders spend a few minutes practicing putting the caps on felt-tipped markers they enjoyed using but routinely forgot to recap. I could not afford to keep replacing the markers when they dried out, so I did a half-humorous lesson on recapping the pens, making sure that we listened for the click that indicated they were on tight (a trick entirely unfamiliar to most of my students). From that point on, the markers seemed to last forever, and the students became remarkably committed to their care.

Building independence and self-management requires more than expectations. We need to encourage initiative and allow kids to behave in ways that they can actually self-manage. This may mean allowing them to get supplies, move about the room, interact with a classmate, or use a certain piece of equipment at specific times without asking permission first. (Having those options can also accommodate the kids' mobility needs as well as their need for autonomy, eliminating a lot of those annoying and attention-getting behaviors we might otherwise see.) Instruction, guidelines, and practice make student responsibility and self-management a reality. Combined with meaningful, positive consequences for cooperation and opportunities to succeed, this type of preparation encourages the positive behaviors that high expectations can indeed inspire.

> Instruction, guidelines, and practice make student responsibility and self-management a reality.

Hot Tips for Increasing Success

- Create a clear mental picture of what you want. Think about any special details or conditions that will be important to you: Do you require a certain heading on the papers they turn in? Will it bother you if someone starts to sharpen a pencil while you're addressing the whole group? Where do you want the materials put when the students are finished with them?
- Identify behaviors and skills your students will need to complete a particular task or function independently and responsibly in your class. Tell your students what you want, preferably before they have a chance to mess up. Let them know how it will benefit them to head their papers a certain way or put materials away properly, for example.
- Assess the levels of ability and self-management your students have already developed. Watch them work—or not work. What happens when you ask them to do routine things in the classroom? Are they able to solve problems on their own? Are they allowed to ask a classmate for assistance when you're not available? Are they bewildered by choices or directions? What does your room look like at the end of the day?
- Assume nothing other than the fact that your students may not be sure what you want—and start from there. Even if they know how to take care of the books in the classroom library, they may not know how *you* want them to do it.
- Have your kids rehearse daily routines. Have them practice moving from their seats to the reading table before you start teaching reading in groups. Have them practice getting equipment and putting these items away before you ask them to do so as part of an activity.
- Have one small group at a time learn to play a game or operate a piece of equipment before they need to use it in a center, a small group activity, or on their own. You often need to train only a handful of kids yourself. Students can learn quickly and well when they know that they will get to train their classmates in turn.
- Unless you intend to spend your entire year guarding, dispensing, and retrieving classroom materials, teach your students how to get, use, and return things when they are finished.
- Whenever possible, make your verbal directions also available in written form.
- Accommodate kinesthetic learners by literally walking them through routines.
- Give instructions in logical sequence. Write complex instructions out, when you can, numbering the steps for clarity.
- In giving verbal directions to young students, low auditory students, or students who have not had much practice developing their listening skills, go slowly, giving directions a step at a time. If possible, wait until the students are ready for the next step before giving them additional information.
- In determining how much information to give out at one time, consider the age and maturity of the students, their experience with your directions, and the complexity of the instructions you have to offer.
- Let your kids know that you're giving them information, even if it's really basic and obvious, only because you want to increase the odds of them being successful, not because you think they're dumb.
- Let the kids monitor the materials. I once decided the best person to keep track of the cards in our individualized handwriting program was the one student who seemed to lose track of them most often. She took her job quite seriously: Not only did she never lose a card after that, but she also once kept the entire class from going to lunch until the "Capital R" card turned up!
- Have the students practice working independently. Assign some seatwork and put yourself off limits while you work at your desk. Make sure the kids have enough to keep them busy, preferably something they can do easily, such as review work, practice drills, or a puzzle. Remember, the emphasis here, for the moment at least, is on building independence—not academic competence.
- Encourage students to help one another or go on to a different task until you are available to help. You'll be amazed at how much progress you can make when your time isn't tied up dealing with behaviors your students can learn to manage on their own.

Use the Activity Checklist to plan or evaluate the directions you assign for various activities.

Activity Checklist

Product and/or Behavior

Objective:

Criteria for successful completion:

Clarity

Skills or behaviors (cognitive, social, motor) required by this activity that may be new to the students:

Materials or equipment used to complete this activity that may be unfamiliar to the students:

Other considerations (for example, movement within or outside the classroom, need for other facilities or resources):

Presentation of Instructions

Verbal:

Written:

Illustrated:

Other (taped, signed, other language):

Samples of finished products available:

Structure

Limits, starting point, or focus:

Choices available:

Other Success-Oriented Features

Getting students' attention:

Time-related (that is, *not* when they're wound up about something else or too far in advance for them to remember):

Small steps:

Logical sequence:

Evaluation Summary

In what ways were these directions success oriented?

In what ways did the students have difficulty with the directions?

In what ways might these directions have been even more success oriented?

Note to self: Next time, remember to . . .

Directions are more meaningful and more likely to engage student cooperation and success when there is a logical reason and benefit to them. Complete Chart 1.1 using the instructions provided.

1. In the first column (or on the left-hand side of a separate piece of paper folded into three columns), list specific behaviors you would like to request from your students.

2. Column 2, identify the primary reason you want them to do what you're asking. Think in terms of logical outcomes ("…so the paste doesn't dry out," " …so the cables don't get tangles," etc.) or benefits to the students, rather than how this would please you, make your life easier, or help the kids avoid an angry or punitive reaction..

3. Column 3, create a request or set of instructions connecting the two: "Let's keep quiet in the hall so we don't bother the other classes." "Please pick the blocks up off the rug so no one trips on them." "Put the CDs back in the case so they don't get scratched." "Get your note in by Tuesday so you can go on the field trip."

Chart 1.1 Developing Clear and Logical Instructions

Desired Behaviors Requested	Reason for Request	Instructions to Student

NOTES

1. How often do we refuse to teach or demonstrate a skill because it's not on our grade level curriculum? As long as I resisted having to teach things they "should have learned by now," I doomed my class, and myself, to needless misunderstanding and misbehavior.

2. See sidebar, "Say It Once!"

3. Adapted from the definition of rubrics on the Ozarka College website: http://www .ozarka.edu/assessment/glossary.cfm.

4. Jo Ann Freiberg, e-mail message to author, February 7, 2006.

CHAPTER TWO

They're Here

Renee Rosenblum-Lowden and
Felicia Lowden Kimmel

THE RUSH TO SEATS

I have a wonderful win-win solution to the awkward first-day rush to find seats. I let students sit where they choose; but as soon as they are seated, I explain that the seating arrangement is not permanent and will be changed. There might be a moan or two, but they usually accept that their seats are temporary. Live with the seating for a couple of days and if it seems to be working, tell them you trust their judgment and you will let them sit where they chose. Suddenly, you are considered the greatest teacher who ever lived because they feel you gave them something. If the seating arrangement has disruptive kids stimulated by other disruptive kids (or a student being intimidated by a nearby classmate), then you go back to your original deal. You are fair because you explained the plan up front, and their moaning will probably be kept to a minimum.

SEATING IDEAS

You can experiment with seating in many ways. There are simple ways, like seating by birthdays, by colors the students are wearing, or by reverse alphabetical order. You can even draw names out of a hat to show that the seating is random. But please don't seat by height or gender (see the next page).

Some people like to cluster their students while others prefer traditional rows. I personally prefer the horseshoe or the upside-down U. Basically, the class is in a semicircle, and I am in the front of the room. There is a trick to this structure that helps with discipline problems. When I first began, I thought I was really clever by putting the disruptive kids on both sides of the room rather than next to one another. *Don't do it!* They'll be facing one another—free to make faces, call out to each other, and act out every other possible human distraction. I finally learned to handle it by seating them all on one side, separated by more attentive students. The challenging kids cannot see one another and are more likely to focus on you. Another advantage is that you can be a physical presence either by standing close to inattentive students or by standing at opposite ends of the room and maintaining eye contact with anyone being disruptive.

If you have a class full of difficult students, I wouldn't try this seating plan; but if there is a good balance of students, this arrangement can get everyone involved in a positive way.

Something I strongly suggest is to rotate your students' seats. I used to do it once a month, and I made sure that they would be seated next to different students. When I did traditional rows, one row would move back a seat, and the next would move down one to assure that someone new was seating next to them. Socialization is very important, and students should be familiar with all their classmates rather than remain in the same cliques.

Don't Seat by Height—Or Gender

It is humiliating for the student who doesn't fit into his or her height "norm" to be singled out for this characteristic. Don't worry about the smaller kids—they can see from anywhere; and if they can't, they will let you know. The last thing a student wants is for you to focus on his or her lack of inches (or abundance thereof—tall kids can feel gawky, too!).

Lining up your students in size order is also not necessary. Try letting them line up by themselves or in alphabetical order (or reverse alphabetical order for those Zieglers who are always last).

Speaking of seating, why is it that we would never segregate children by race, yet we insist on segregating by gender? Even if it is what the students prefer, we as educators have got to stop perpetuating the myth that males and females are "opposites." We have to foster inter-action as early as possible and to not let each sex see the other one as "the enemy" or "the other." Perhaps if we stop separating children by gender in the earlier grades, boys and girls will become more enriched by each other by the time they enter the middle grades.

DEALING FOR GROUPS

Using a deck of playing cards is a good strategy for assigning groups when they don't have to be balanced by academic performance. What I suggest is to try to make as many different combinations as possible during the year, and that can be done simply enough by giv-ing students playing cards and taping them to their book bags. (You should jot down which card each student has so if one of them loses his card, you have your own record.) If there are 28 students, you hand out ace through 7 of all suits.

If you want a large group, you can call the suit. If you want small groups, you can call the same number. If you want more than four, you can pick two numbers. If you are ambitious and want to mix it up, you can pick numbers and suits (red aces, black threes). There are endless combinations. One of the advantages of this is that your students will know early on that the grouping is random, and you should also let them know that you will not tolerate groaning if a student they don't like joins the group.

RECORD KEEPING QUESTIONNAIRE

You will need lots of information from your students and their parents. A good idea is to have a questionnaire ready for them to fill out along with one for their parents. You should include your students' names, addresses, phone numbers, and e-mail addresses along with their schedules so you can find them in the event that you need to reach them. You can ask for their extracurricular activities and find out if they work after school. Parents should give you their work phone numbers and their availability during the day. You can ask parents if they have any skills they would be willing to share with your class. It is also a good idea to ask what language is spoken at home. You might also include a question about things that parents want to ask you. Giving parents an opportunity to ask you questions in advance of parent teacher conferences might enable you to give them thoughtful answers. You might even offer suggestion questions such as "Have you noticed any behavioral changes? What can we do together to make sure my child has a great year?"

When you have all this information returned to you, put it in a large binder; and if you are feeling particularly organized that week, you might buy tab pages that have pockets in them. Now you have a binder with every student's name and pertinent information. Keep conference notes, conversations with parents and counselors, referral slips, and so on in this binder; therefore, everything will be organized and easy to find if you need to refer to it.

Now and Later Cards

Now and Later Cards first introduce the students to you at the beginning of the year and later show how they have changed by the end of the year.

You begin by giving out small index cards and composing questions that will give you insight about your students. Examples might include the following:

What is your favorite subject?

What is your pet peeve?

What do you hope will happen to you this year?

What music do you like?

Save the cards and on the last day of school, return the cards to them. They always laugh because half of the answers hardly describe them at the end of the year. I have seen teens cringe because they liked the "wrong" rock group in September and can't believe how uncool they were.

The First Day "Sneaker"

A wonderful first day activity for younger children is to place an array of materials on each student's desk. The packet holding the materials could be in the shape of a sneaker and called "Stepping Into the Fifth Grade Sneaker." Having simple tasks on their desks lets them get started without having to ask for directions, gives them something to do right away, and hopefully sets the tone for the rest of the year. To make it really special, you can write each student's name on his or her "sneaker."

FUN INTRODUCTIONS

Depending on the age of your students, there are many ways they can introduce themselves. I'll just throw a few at you.

Younger children can say their names and add a noun, as in "Sarah the Singer." When you do this, please don't make children repeat all the names said before them. This is very stressful to kids and unfair to the last child. Another way is to have kids reveal one thing that is special about them (or makes them different from others in your class). Students can pair up and find out as much as they can about one another and then introduce their partners. Some students simply find it is easier to talk about others rather than about themselves. This exercise might be easier if you have a prepared list of suggested questions. Another pairing strategy is to have each two-some list a few things they have in common and a few ways in which they are totally different from one another. If there is an odd number of students, go ahead and jump in and be the other half of a pair. A really fun exercise is to have each child write one truth about himself and one lie and have the class guess which is which. It's a good ice-breaker because the kids love it and it is easy for you to take part. If you feel more comfortable with traditional methods, you can give them a written assignment wherein they introduce themselves on paper and read what they wrote aloud. This is also a subtle way to assess their writing skills.

PUT YOUR NAME—AND PHONE NUMBER?—ON THE BOARD

Needless to say, your name goes on the board *first thing*. Since you are the boss, it's really important that they know who you are. But you're probably asking, "Why in heaven's name would I give these total strangers my home phone number?" You probably have visions of half the school calling and asking if your refrigerator is running and then telling you to go catch it! There may be those who would actually do that, but the amazing discovery I've made is that when they have permission to call, they usually don't unless it is school related.

I do this for two reasons. First, they feel it is such an act of trust that you would actually let them call you at home. I make it very clear that they may call only if it is very important and they must speak to me. They may not call about homework assignments because they have a homework buddy for that. (See Homework Buddies on page 43.) I also explain that I go to bed early and not to call after 9 o'clock. Second, I am so generous with my number because if they wanted to make a prank call, all they'd have to do is look my number up in the phone book!

In the beginning there are usually a few kids who will call on a pretense just to hear my "at-home" voice. Occasionally, I've gotten calls from kids in crisis. Very seldom did I get "mystery calls," and the few that I did get may have been students or just people dialing a wrong number and not using proper phone etiquette.

This is just my experience. Many teachers are not comfortable with this and therefore should not do it. (It's easy not to if your name is Smith!)

YOU'VE GOT MAIL

Okay, so you do not want to give your students your telephone number. However, there is another way to communicate with them outside of school—through the Internet. Now that most schools have an e-mail address for each teacher, your students and their parents can ask you questions or express concerns and you can respond in 100 words or less.

Some teachers give their students their personal e-mail address, but let me warn you what can happen if you are on their buddy list. You suddenly hear the ping of an "instant message," and then another and then another, and suddenly you are aware that your entire class wants to chat online. Consider using a different screen name so all you have to do is switch your screen name and your students will not know that you are surfing the Net planning your vacation.

TANGIBLE CLASS GUIDELINES AND RULES

It is important that you think through what you expect from your class and what they should expect from you. You can explain everything to them in detail, but it helps to have the rules in writing and in their hands (and on the bulletin board). You can give them two sets. The first must be kept in their notebooks, and the other they and their parents must sign and return to you to keep on file. During the year, when a student says, "I didn't know you would fail me because I didn't do 188 homework assignments," you can pull out her signed agreement. It is important that the parents sign this agreement because some parents have been known to try to put teachers on the defensive, saying they were not informed of certain requirements their child had to fulfill. You can show them the signed contract and this usually ends the confrontation.

LET STUDENTS SET RULES AND CONSEQUENCES

You can ask the class what rules they consider fair. (Don't ask what rules they think are unfair—if you do, you'll be sorry!)

For instance, I ask them what would make a classroom feel safe, and then we brainstorm and compile a list of rules. It is hard for them to complain that the rules they set are unfair.

Of course, if you see that they are not being serious and are making rules such as "There should be no homework ever," go back to a dictatorship and declare yourself czar.

YOU OWN THE LIMELIGHT

The beginning of the school year is the time to establish yourself as the person in charge.

Observe how peer groups form and how you sometimes unwittingly become part of this process. I have seen some kids be perceived as "cool" if they can put down the teacher. If they are successful, you're in big trouble. Common behavior patterns of this kind of student are to yell out to the teacher, mutter under his breath, or just engage other kids in a conversation while you are right there at the front of the room being just as nice as you can be. What to do?

Sometimes a quick glance at the disruptive student may suffice. If not, you may have to do the unthinkable, and that might involve embarrassing the student. Stop and explain to the "cool" kid that under no circumstances do you talk over anyone else and that you will protect that right for everyone in the room. (To some, this can be terribly intimidating.)

If you talk over a conversation, the noise level just rises; and before you know it, no one can be heard and you are yelling. I am not saying that a classroom should always be quiet—I would hardly want that—but when the lesson is teacher directed, the teacher has the floor.

Good educational experiences usually encourage enthusiastic talking, and that is music to the ears.

You Can Always Ease Up

It is tempting to be permissive from the beginning because no one wants to start out the year with all those "mean" rules. But unless you establish them early on, you will pay the consequences. If you say there will be homework every day, they will groan but expect it. On the day you give them no homework, you'll be seen as a saint.

But the reverse can be catastrophic. Try telling kids you won't give them homework on the weekends and then do just the opposite. You will have a potential student revolution on your hands.

Sit With Your Students

Too often we stand in front of the room and just lecture. It can be boring and sometimes even a little intimidating; but alas, that's where the blackboard or the overhead is, and standing there brings the focus to you. But on occasion, I pull up a chair and sit with my students, usually while reading a story or having a class discussion. Sitting at their level makes everyone feel more comfortable. I have found that this strategy encourages more students to participate.

Also, sitting on top of a desk, rather than standing, accomplishes the same thing and puts off your need to purchase those less attractive "sensible shoes."

GREET STUDENTS AT THE DOOR

Very often our students feel alienated in school, especially older students who travel from teacher to teacher. They are often one of hundreds of students in a building and rarely get individual recognition unless they are outstanding in some way.

Teachers should always be ready to teach and be waiting for their students. Why not greet them at the door? What is really special is greeting them by name. One colleague of mine who taught ninth graders would refer to his students by their surnames, which made them feel they were treated like respected adults.

DOCUMENT! DOCUMENT! DOCUMENT!

When there is an accident or a major infraction, teachers must put it in writing and on record. Make sure your statements are nonjudgmental and contain only the facts without personal interpretation.

Sometimes, because we are so overwhelmed with all our responsibilities as a teacher, we put off writing the report and forget about it. Try not to. Very often parents will side with their child no matter what and will accuse you of picking on the student. It is helpful if a teacher is able to retrieve a file and show parents that the child has past offenses that are documented. According to law, you must document accidents because lawsuits are becoming increasingly common. Basically, I am just telling you to protect yourself.

I had this horrendously disruptive and hurtful child in my class. When I spoke to the mother, she initially expressed concern. As time went by her concern shifted to "getting the teachers" rather than getting help for her son. He had set a fire in the bathroom, and all she wanted to see was the documentation. Rather than address the serious issues regarding her son's behavior, she would put me on the defensive. I was stunned to see how few teachers had written up reports on him (though we would share "Jimmy" stories over lunch, trying to find solutions to help him). This mother attacked me verbally, saying I just didn't like her child. (More about those parents later.) Had I had all the documentation, I might have been able to get this child help. He eventually ended up getting hurt by another student instead of getting the counseling he desperately needed.

Yowks! Five Minutes Left

It was bound to happen. You had it perfectly planned—a 40-minute lesson for your 30-minute time slot. But guess what? It bombed! You lost their interest, you tried every trick in the book to resuscitate your lesson, and you found that you still had time to spare. Not enough time to start something new, but too much time to sit and wait for the bell to ring.

What to do? I don't care what grade you're teaching: Play Simon Says. It's a sure crowd pleaser. If you want to be more cerebral, play Hangman, and to make sure they enjoy it, divide the room in half and make it a team competition. My Hangman game is always a sentence rather than a word. (It depends on how many minutes you have left to ad lib!) Reading a story that can be picked up at any point is another good idea. You know you have a winner when the bell rings and they groan.

End the First Day on an Up Note

Make sure the day ends on a positive note. You may have told them about the term projects they will be getting and given them lots of books to take home to cover. But today you can be so kind by announcing that they will have only a short assignment because you want them to be well rested for a great day tomorrow. Your day ends, hopefully, with smiling students who feel you are the fairest person in the world and who will be indebted to you forever—okay, maybe not forever, but a few hours are better than nothing!

Chapter 3

Handling Social Misbehavior

David A. Sousa

THE SOCIAL AND EMOTIONAL BRAIN

"I was so angry, I couldn't think straight!" "He got me so mad, I nearly hit him!" Both of these statements make it clear that emotions were running high. Human beings have been interacting with emotions for thousands of years, but understanding where they come from and how they direct our behavior is still not fully understood. Nevertheless, thanks to the development of brain imaging techniques, researchers have made substantial progress in discovering the underlying neural networks that encourage and inhibit certain behaviors. After all, we are not just information processing machines. We are also motivated, social, and emotional beings who are constantly interacting with our environment. Schools and classrooms are particularly demanding environments because so many different personalities gather together in a confined area where they are expected to interact according to established rules of accepted emotional and social behavior.

> Schools and classrooms are demanding environments because so many different personalities gather together in a confined area where they are expected to interact according to established rules of accepted emotional and social behavior.

So what is happening inside the brain of students who display socially unacceptable behavior? Are these just temporary responses to a particular situation or are they symptoms of an underlying disorder? Do we immediately refer the student for mental evaluation or try a classroom intervention that may improve the behavior? These are difficult questions. But before we can answer them, we need to review some of what scientists know about how emotions are processed in the brain. The purpose here is not to make educators into neuroscientists. But the more teachers know about how the emotional brain works, the more likely they are to choose instructional strategies that will lead to appropriate student behavior and successful student achievement.

Emotional Processing

Long before the advent of brain imaging technology, researchers in the 1950s suggested that the structures responsible for processing emotions were located in the mid-brain, an area that Paul MacLean (1952) described as the *limbic system* (Figure 3.1). His work was very influential and the term "limbic system" persisted and continues to show up in modern texts on the brain. However, current research does not support the notion that the limbic system is the only area where emotions are processed, or that all the structures in the limbic system are dedicated to emotions. Brain imaging shows that the frontal lobe and other regions are also activated when emotions are processed, and limbic structures such as the hippocampus are involved in nonemotional processes, such as memory. In light of these newer discoveries, the trend now is to refer to this location as the "limbic area," as we have in Figure 3.1.

MacLean also described the *frontal lobe* (lying just behind the forehead) as the area where thinking occurs. We now know that the frontal lobe comprises the rational and executive control center of the brain, processing higher-order thinking and directing problem solving. In addition, one of its most important functions is to use cognitive processing to monitor and control the emotions generated by limbic structures. In this role, the frontal lobe is supposed to keep us from doing things when we are angry that we would regret later, and from taking unnecessary risks just to indulge emotional curiosity or please others.

Development of the Brain's Emotional and Rational Areas

Among other things, human survival depends on the family unit, where emotional bonds increase the chances of producing children and raising them to be productive adults. The human brain has learned over thousands of years that survival and emotional messages must have high priority when it filters through all the incoming signals from the body's senses. So it is no surprise that studies of human brain growth show that the emotional (and biologically older) regions develop faster and mature much earlier than the frontal lobes (Paus, 2005; Steinberg, 2005). Figure 3.2 shows the approximate percent development of the brain's limbic area and frontal lobes from birth through the age of 24 years. The limbic area is fully mature around the age of 10 to 12 years, but the frontal lobes mature closer to 22 to 24 years of age. Consequently, the emotional system is more likely to win the tug-of-war for control of behavior during the preadolescent years.

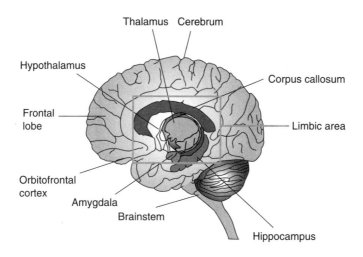

Figure 3.1   A cross section of the human brain showing major structures and highlighting the limbic area buried deep within the brain.

What does this mean in a classroom of preadolescents? Emotional messages guide their behavior, including directing their attention to a learning situation. Specifically, emotion drives attention and attention drives learning. But even more important to understand is that emotional attention comes *before* cognitive recognition. For instance, you see a snake in the garden and within a few seconds your palms are sweating, your breathing is labored, and your blood pressure is rising—all this before you know whether the snake is even alive. That's your limbic area acting without input from the cognitive parts of the brain (frontal lobe). Thus, the brain is responding emotionally to a situation that could be potentially life-threatening without the benefit of cognitive functions, such as thinking, reasoning, and consciousness (Damasio, 2003).

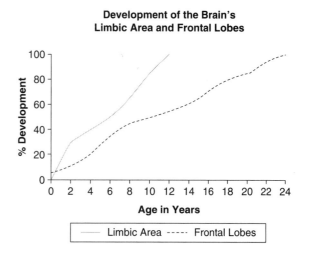

Figure 3.2   Based on recent studies, this chart suggests the possible degree of development of the brain's limbic area and frontal lobes.

Source: Adapted from Paus, 2005, and Steinberg, 2005.

Preadolescents are likely to respond emotionally to a situation much faster than rationally. Obviously, this emotional predominance can easily get them into trouble. If two students bump into each other in the school corridor, one of them may just as likely respond with a retaliatory punch than with a "sorry." On the positive side, this emotional focus can have an advantage when introducing a lesson. Getting the students' attention for a lesson will be more successful when they make an emotional link to the day's learning objective. Starting a lesson with "Today we are going to study fractions" will not capture their focus anywhere near as fast as asking whether they would rather have one-third, one-fourth, or one-sixth of a pizza. Whenever a teacher attaches a positive emotion to the lesson, it not only gets attention but it also helps the students to see real-life applications.

The Orbitofrontal Cortex: The Decision Maker

As investigations into emotions have become more extensive, it is clear that emotions are a complex behavior that cannot be assigned to a single neural system. Instead, different neural systems are likely to be activated, depending on the emotional task or situation. These systems might involve regions that are primarily specialized for emotional processing as well as regions that serve other purposes. However, two brain areas whose prime function appears to be processing emotions are the *orbitofrontal cortex* and the *amygdala* (Gazzaniga, Ivry, & Mangun, 2002).

The orbitofrontal cortex is at the base of the frontal lobe and rests on the upper wall of the orbit above the eyes (Figure 3.1). Research of this brain area indicates that it regulates our abilities to evaluate, inhibit, and act on social and emotional information. Exactly how this regulating effect works is still not fully understood, but imaging studies continue to provide clues. Brain scans reveal that a neural braking mechanism is activated for a few milliseconds (a millisecond is 1/1,000th of a second) when adults are asked to make a decision based mainly on an emotional stimulus. The braking signal is sent to a region near the thalamus (see Figure 3.1) which stops motor movement. A third brain region initiates the plan to halt or continue a response. The

> *The brain's frontal cortex activates a braking mechanism that halts movement for a few milliseconds to allow an individual to decide what action to take in response to an emotional stimulus.*

signals among these brain areas travel very fast because they are directly connected to each other. In this process, putting on the brakes may provide just enough time for the individual to make a more rational and less emotional decision (Aron, Behrens, Smith, Frank, & Poldrack, 2007). However, the less mature the regulating mechanisms are, the less effective this braking process can be. As a result, the abilities regulated by the systems in the orbitofrontal cortex essentially form the decisions we make regarding our social and emotional behavior.

Social Decision Making. One way in which we make decisions is to analyze incoming and internal information within a social context and then decide what action to take. For example, we might be so upset by something that we just want to shout out a cry of disgust. But if at that moment we are riding on a packed bus or walking through a crowded shopping mall, the social context (Will these people think I'm insane?) inhibits us from doing so. In schools, students often refrain from doing what they really want

> *Social context is a powerful inhibitor or encourager of behavior.*

for fear of what their peers will think of their behavior. For instance, some students regrettably do not perform to their potential in school because they fear that their peers will think of them as nerds or teacher's pets and thus ostracize them from their social group. On the other hand, students sometimes perform risky behaviors (e.g., underage drinking, reckless driving) just to get their peers' attention. Social context, therefore, is a powerful inhibitor or encourager of behavior.

People with damage to the orbitofrontal region have difficulty inhibiting inappropriate social behavior, such as unprovoked aggressiveness, and have problems in making social decisions. Also, although they fully understand the purposes of physical objects around them, they often use them in socially inappropriate ways. For example, a student with this deficit knows well that a pencil is for writing, but may be using it to repeatedly poke others.

Emotional Decision Making. Because social cues often give us emotional feedback, how we act in a social context cannot easily be separated from how we evaluate and act on emotional information. Nonetheless, experimental evidence suggests that the orbitofrontal cortex evaluates the type of emotional response that is appropriate for a particular situation. Sometimes, this means modifying what would normally be an automatic response. For example, think of a toddler eyeing a plate of chocolate chip cookies. If the child is not allowed to have one, the frustration could well cause the child to throw a fit and physically display anger by kicking and screaming. His brain's frontal lobes have not developed sufficiently to moderate the impulse. Thus the child readily shares his emotions with everyone around him. Now an older child in the same situation might feel like throwing a fit but his frontal cortex has developed further and moderates the impulses. Head injury, abuse, alcoholism, and other traumatic events can interfere with the brain's ability to moderate emotions, resulting in a more primitive level of behavior inconsistent with the child's age.

Here's another example. We generally laugh out loud at a really funny joke. But doing so, say, at a lecture or in church would not be the emotionally appropriate action. Thus, the orbitofrontal cortex quickly evaluates the social situation and overrides the typical response of loud laughter (Rolls, 1999). To perform this function successfully, the orbitofrontal cortex has to rely on learned information from other brain structures. One of those structures that interacts with the orbitofrontal cortex is the amygdala.

The Amygdala: A Gateway for Emotional Learning

The amygdala (Greek for "almond," because of its shape and size) is located in the limbic area just in front of the hippocampus, one in each of the brain's two hemispheres (Figure 3.1). Figure 3.3 shows the location of the amygdala on each side of the brain. Numerous studies have indicated that the amygdala is important for emotional learning and memory. These learnings can be related to implicit emotional learning, explicit memory, social responses, and vigilance. Let's briefly explain each of these.

Implicit Emotional Learning. Suppose a student lives in a neighborhood where gang shootings are not unusual. The sound of gunfire produces fear in the student. If the student hears a car backfire in the school parking lot, that same fear reaction will occur. That's because the student's amygdala has associated a neutral stimulus (car backfiring) with a fearful event (a gun shot). This implicit learning has resulted in what is called *fear conditioning.* Someone coming upon a snarling dog would have a similar reaction. Information from the visual processing system would activate the amygdala which would immediately send signals to the brain stem to increase heart rate and blood pressure as well as to the frontal lobe to decide what action to take.

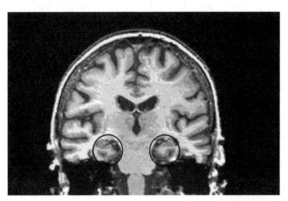

Figure 3.3 The circles show the location of the amygdala in the brain's left and right hemispheres.

Explicit Emotional Learning and Memory. The amygdala interacts with other memory components, particularly its neighbor, the *hippocampus* (Figure 3.1). The hippocampus (Greek for "sea horse," because of its shape) is situated in the limbic area just behind the amygdala in each of the brain's hemispheres. It is an integral part of the brain's memory systems and thought to be mainly involved in encoding cognitive and spatial information into long-term memory.

Information stored in long-term memory can activate the amygdala and cause a fear response to a situation even though the individual has not encountered that exact situation in the past. For example, imagine John, a middle-school student, walking to school and seeing another student coming toward him. As the other student draws near, John gets nervous and fearful and crosses to the other side of the street. What caused this response? It could very well be that John heard from one of his friends that the other student is a bully who gets into fights without provocation. Now, John has had no bad experiences with the bully, but learned about his aggressiveness explicitly from a friend, and that information was stored through the hippocampal memory system.

It is unlikely that John experienced fear when he was told the information. However, when he saw the bully walking toward him, the memory of the information alerted the amygdala, which provoked the fear response. This type of emotional learning, whereby we avoid or fear a situation because of what we are told rather than because of our own experience, is common in humans.

Of course, we remember some emotional experiences because they gave us good feelings: our first kiss, the pride we felt at graduation, our wedding day. The amygdala's interaction with the hippocampal memory system ensures that we remember things that are emotionally important for a long time, while also remembering those situations that can be threatening.

Teachers can use this information to enhance the impact of their teaching. Whenever a teacher can identify a strong emotional tie-in to the lesson content, and explicitly address that emotional connection while teaching, the content is likely to be recalled much longer and with greater clarity by most students. For

> *Whenever a teacher can identify a strong emotional tie-in to the lesson content, that content is likely to be recalled much longer and with greater clarity by most students.*

example, when teaching about the era of segregation in a U.S. History class, the teacher might want to begin by saying to the students, "Anyone wearing white tennis shoes has to sit in the back of the class today, and you cannot eat in the cafeteria at lunch! Please move to the back of the class now!" The teacher would then move those students. Next the teacher inquires how those statements and their forced move to the back made them feel. Finally, the teacher explains that some citizens of the United States were treated in such a poor fashion because of the color of their skin. It is likely that this example generates strong emotions in many readers, and therefore will be remembered much longer.

Social Responses. Although the role of the amygdala in social processing is limited, it does seem to be important in evaluating facial and vocal expressions. Brain imaging studies indicate that the amygdala on the left side of the brain responds more to voice information, and the amygdala on the right side is more involved processing facial expressions. These studies further demonstrate that the amygdala shows activation with different types of emotional expressions, such as happy or angry (Johnstone, van Reekum, Oakes, & Davidson, 2006). However, the activation is particularly intense when responding to fearful facial expressions. This response extends also to evaluating other social judgments about faces, such as deciding from a facial expression whether or not a person in a picture seems approachable or trustworthy (Adolphs, Tranel, & Denburg, 2000).

Such sensitivity to facial and emotional expressions is important for teachers to remember. No matter what we say to students, if the amygdala's assessment of our facial expressions and emotional demeanor contradicts our words, then they will probably not believe us. As a consequence, the teacher-student trust relationship is eroded.

Vigilance. It has long been thought that the amygdala not only processes an emotional stimulus, but also causes the emotional *response* to that stimulus. However, more recent research indicates that the amygdala's role seems to be to process emotional information and to *alert* other brain regions that should be sensitive to this information. Apparently, the amygdala increases the vigilance of other cerebral systems so that they can respond to the situation, if necessary (Anderson & Phelps, 2002).

Pathways of Emotional Signals

The *thalamus* is a limbic area structure that receives all incoming sensory impulses (except smell) and directs them to other parts of the brain for further processing. Incoming sensory

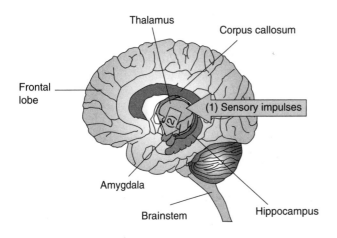

Figure 3.4 In the thalamic pathway, sensory impulses (1) travel to the thalamus where they are routed directly to the amygdala (2).

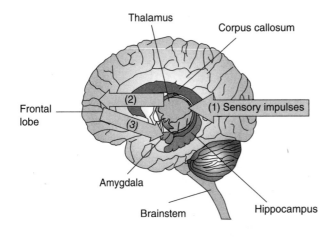

Figure 3.5 In the cortical pathway, sensory impulses (1) are routed first to the frontal lobe (2) for cognitive processing and then on to the amygdala (3).

information to the thalamus that has an emotional component can take two different routes to the amygdala. The quick route (called the *thalamic pathway*) sends the signals directly from the thalamus to the amygdala, as shown in Figure 3.4. The second possibility (called the *cortical pathway*) is for the thalamus to direct the signals first to the frontal lobe for cognitive processing and then to the amygdala, as shown in Figure 3.5.

The time it takes for signals to travel along the two pathways is different. For example, it takes sound signals about 12 milliseconds to travel the thalamic pathway and about twice as long to travel the cortical pathway. Which pathway the signals take could mean the difference between life and death. If the sound from an approaching car blasting its horn travels along the thalamic pathway, it will probably be fast enough to get you to jump out of the way even though you are not sure what is coming. Only later does your frontal lobe provide the explanation of what happened. Survival is the first priority; the explanation can wait.

Disturbances or deficits in this dual pathway system can explain some abnormal social behaviors. Social anxiety disorders, for example, can result whenever a certain action, such as walking into a crowd, is associated with fear. If this activity always takes the faster thalamic pathway, there is no opportunity for the frontal lobe to reassure you that there is no need for fear. Without that input, a phobia develops that cannot be easily moderated later through rational discussion. This probably explains why psychotherapy alone is seldom successful in treating many phobias and anxiety disorders (Restak, 2000;

Schneier, 2003). Treatments now often combine medication with psychotherapy. The principal medications used for anxiety disorders are antidepressants, antianxiety drugs, and beta-blockers to control some of the physical symptoms. Alternative therapies, such as diet modification, eye movement desensitization and reprocessing, and relaxation techniques have also been successful with some individuals. With proper treatment, many people with anxiety disorders can lead normal, fulfilling lives.

What Leads to Social Misbehavior?

Sociologists have examined for decades the various factors that influence how people behave in social situations. Children, of course, often behave quite differently from adults in similar situations, largely because their social skills are still developing. Further, as we discussed earlier, their frontal lobe's executive control system is immature and not yet fully capable of constraining excessive emotional responses.

The neurobiology of social behavior and misbehavior is not well understood. However, the new field of social neuroscience is emerging and some exciting avenues of research are being explored. The goal is to understand social behavior from the perspective of the brain. By using brain-imaging techniques and studies of people with brain injuries, researchers hope to decipher how neural pathways control attitudes, stereotypes, emotions and other socially motivated phenomena.

As exciting as brain imaging is, it does have its limits. People in a scanner cannot move very much and they do not usually interact directly with other people. The signals, by themselves, do not indicate a specific behavior. But these brain signals must be linked with behavior to have psychological meaning. Furthermore, the results of imaging studies must be associated with findings in other related areas, such as lesion studies, animal studies, and studies involving pharmaceuticals. With this approach in mind, research teams have begun examining areas of social behavior such as *stereotyping* and *attitudes*.

Stereotyping. In earlier studies, social psychologists have found that the brain automatically places people and objects into categories such as "familiar" and "foreign," and "good" and "bad." This categorization then biases an individual's feelings and reactions toward those people and objects. Not surprisingly, neuroscientists used imaging technology to focus on the amygdala to put together a possible neural pathway that might lead to stereotyping. One question they asked was "Does this brain structure consider people of different races as emotionally important?" They discovered that the amygdala is especially active at the sight of any unfamiliar face. However, once it has seen these faces several times, it stops emphasizing faces of people of the same race and only emphasizes more the sight of faces of a different race. Thus, the amygdala in whites is more active when they look at black faces, and in blacks it is more active when they look at white faces. This increased activity in the amygdala *could* evoke a fear response and subconsciously strengthen stereotypes about people of different races (Hart et al., 2000).

These results do not mean that there is a brain module for racial categories. It is more probably the result of environmental experiences during our development as a species. Our early ancestors did not get around very much and thus had no opportunity to encounter people who looked different from themselves. When they did encounter others, their brain circuits classified them as to whether they were likely to be an ally or an enemy.

Furthermore, the increased amygdala activity does not mean the response is unchangeable. New experiences change the brain. A follow-up imaging study revealed that the response of the amygdala to same-race versus other-race faces was altered by familiarity and learning (Phelps et al., 2000). In other words, just because we see the representation of a behavior in the brain does not lessen the importance of learning on generating or changing that behavior (Kurzban, Tooby, & Cosmides, 2001; Phelps & Thomas, 2003).

Attitudes. Researchers have long thought that an individual can change attitude after some amount of conscious reprocessing of information. Cognitive dissonance theory, for example, predicts that people change their attitudes after consciously realizing that there is a conflict between their core beliefs and their attitudes. Studies have used patients with amnesia to examine pathways that might be involved in changing attitudes. The researchers found that people with amnesia show an even bigger tendency to change their attitudes when shown a conflict between their attitudes and their beliefs than do people without amnesia. Cognitive dissonance theory would not have predicted this result because people with amnesia cannot remember long enough to realize consciously that a conflict exists (Ochsner & Lieberman, 2001).

However, when you think about it from the perspective of the brain, this finding does make sense. The brain consists of many automatic processes that respond unconsciously to the context of any situation facing the individual. When people with amnesia are told that their attitude conflicts with their core beliefs, their brain automatically changes the attitude to coincide with the beliefs. The only difference is that these individuals do not have access to the conscious processes, such as pride, that might stop them from going through with the change.

The implications of these findings can be applied to schools. Students with social and emotional problems often have distorted and negative attitudes and stereotypes about their family, school, peers, or even themselves. These attitudes and stereotypes may indeed be in conflict with their core beliefs, but they have not had the opportunity to do the cognitive reflection necessary to recognize that this conflict exists. Interventions, therefore, that help students reflect on their misbehavior and on the degree to which that misbehavior is directed by their attitudes and stereotypes are likely to be successful.

This cognitive reflection on one's awareness of and ability to manage one's emotions in a healthy and productive manner is known as *emotional intelligence.* Redenbach (2004) suggests that teaching emotional intelligence involves heightening the students' awareness of their feelings and the connection between their feelings and their actions. This instruction focuses on showing students the powerful choices they make when deciding how to act on their emotions. The result is an increase in the students' ability to manage their emotions successfully in a variety of situations.

With this approach, teachers help students to become experts in the five steps to emotional intelligence: self-awareness, mood management, motivation, empathy, and social skills. Accomplishing this requires the students to gain the ability to do the following:

- Accurately perceive, appraise, and express emotion
- Access or generate feelings on demand when they can facilitate understanding of themselves or another person
- Understand emotions and the knowledge that derives from them
- Regulate emotions to promote emotional and intellectual growth

The important point to be made here is that regardless of the basic cause of social misbehavior, most individuals can *learn* to moderate their behavior through appropriate interventions. Obviously, the sooner these interventions occur, the better. Numerous studies have shown that middle school students who display disruptive and antisocial behavior are at high risk for achieving poorly in high school and becoming dropouts (Battin-Pearson et al., 2000; Newcomb et al., 2002). But there is good news. The research studies also show that if interventions in elementary and middle schools can reduce forms of disruptive and antisocial behavior, then the students' chances for academic success in high school increase significantly (Fleming et al., 2005). These preventive interventions work with elementary

> *Regardless of the basic cause of social misbehavior, most individuals can learn to moderate their behavior through appropriate interventions.*

and middle school students to develop healthy peer relationships and avoid the influence of peers engaged in problem behaviors. Research studies have found programs such as the *Life Skills Training Program* (Botvin & Griffin, 2004), *Project Alert* (Ellickson, McCaffrey, Ghosh-Dastidar, & Longshore, 2003), and *All Stars* (McNeal, Hansen, Harrington, & Giles, 2004) to be effective.

The Teacher Is the Key

Once again, the classroom teacher becomes a key person in deciding how to deal with students who display inappropriate social and emotional behavior. We know from studies that elementary teachers regard certain social and self-control skills as essential for the students' success in their classroom. In one study, more than 125 elementary teachers identified the following seven social skills as being pivotal for student success in their classroom (Lane, Givner, & Pierson, 2004):

- Following directions
- Attending to instructions
- Controlling temper with peers

- Controlling temper with adults
- Getting along with people
- Responding appropriately when hit
- Using free time acceptably

Elementary teachers (and probably many of their colleagues in secondary schools) value skills that promote harmony in the classroom and want to minimize assertive behaviors that could be challenging or disruptive. Teachers, of course, are not diagnosticians or therapists, but they are keen observers. They can certainly recognize when a student's behavioral problems persist and escalate, and they can decide what options to choose. One of those options is to try with interventions that research studies support as effective in controlling student behavior. Here are few of those interventions aimed at controlling social misbehavior.

INTERVENTIONS FOR HANDLING SOCIAL MISBEHAVIOR

We have already seen that social misbehavior can arise for a number of reasons. Handling such misbehavior requires careful assessment of the situation to determine which interventions are likely to be most effective. Here are a few suggestions that include dealing with interventions that target social anxieties as well as those that use social stories to curb undesirable social behavior.

Dealing With Social Anxieties

Researchers in social neuroscience offer suggestions for dealing with students who have social anxieties because these are often an indication of potential misbehavior in social situations. The following suggestions are from the schoolpsychiatry.org website of the Department of Psychiatry at Massachusetts General Hospital (copyright MGH, 2006), and are included here with permission. With modifications, these interventions are appropriate for students at all grade levels. See the **Resources** section for more information about the material available from this source.

- **Using puppets with primary students.** Allow socially anxious children to practice social encounters—such as initiating, sustaining, and concluding a conversation—with puppets. You may need a script for some students. For example, "Hi, I'm Bunny the Rabbit. What's your name? I like to eat carrots. What do you like to eat? Where do you like to play? I have to go now. Thanks for talking with me. Goodbye."
- **Watching social encounters.** Some preadolescents and adolescents have little understanding of what to do in a social encounter. Ask the student to watch videos that include social encounters and to identify what others did to be comfortable. What did the video characters

do with their eyes? How did they move their hands and feet while talking to others? How did the others react? And how did the student feel while observing the character?

- **Helping the resistant contributor.** Some students speak off-task freely but resist speaking about the lesson topic for fear of making mistakes in front of their peers. Allow these students to observe several other students before attempting a task. They should observe how other students start speaking, how long they speak, where they look, and how they stop. Then have the reluctant student speak to a group of three or four familiar peers before presenting to the whole class.

- **Sitting with familiar or preferred peers.** Identify peers that the student feels safe sitting close to and place some students into close proximity. Guide the student about how to talk to peers about assignments, such as "How many assignments do we have? When are they due? Where do we start?"

- **Identifying a student helper.** Matching a reluctant or overbearing student with a specific peer or peers can often help that student demonstrate acceptable behavior and participate in class. If the student does not know an answer when called on, allow the student to select a "lifeline." This is a peer whom the student believes will know the correct answer. If the student uses a lifeline, do not accept the answer until the student using the lifeline states whether the lifeline's answer is correct.

- **Sharing feelings.** Adults and peers are often so busy dealing with a student's social misbehavior that they rarely stop and have a face-to-face talk about what is going on. Identify specific times when the student can share feelings with you or another staff person or peer.

- **Rehearsing social skills.** Some socially misbehaving students simply need practice in what constitutes *acceptable* behavior. In a small group facilitated by a counselor, ask the students to review and role play how to make and keep friends. Give students homework to practice the social skills in other settings, such as the classroom, playground, and at home. Then pick frequent or familiar social situations—such as establishing rules in playground games, buying groceries, ordering at a restaurant, asking others to play soccer—and allow the student to role play with other students.

- **Practicing self-monitoring.** Identify and practice steps for the student to self-monitor appropriate peer interactions. For example, "Am I letting other people talk, too? Are we taking turns? Am I learning something from this conversation?"

- **Examining the evidence of negative conclusions.** If the student says, "I can't go to gym class because everyone will laugh at me," ask the student, "What happened the last time you went to gym class? Did any good things happen last time?" Or the student might say, "I don't like coming to school because people make fun of me." Ask the student, "What do students do when they arrive at school? Which students are glad to see you?"

- **Identifying automatic negative thoughts.** The student says, "I act out to get other students' attention because I'm no fun. No one wants to be around (or play with) me." Ask the student, "What happened that made you think this?" or "What causes you to think this?"

Using Social Stories to Modify Behavior

Because of the impressive influence of peers on most students, teachers should consider using behavioral strategies that employ both the power of the social context to modify problem behaviors, as well as teach tactics to curb emotional outbursts. This approach is useful for both general and special education teachers.

The use of social stories—sometimes referred to as *comic strip conversations*—addresses both of these factors, and has received considerable research support (Agosta, Graetz, Mastropieri, & Scruggs, 2004; Haggerty, Black, & Smith, 2005; Parsons, 2006; Rogers & Myles, 2001). A social story is a brief story that presents a problem behavior and various potential consequences of that behavior in a social context. Social stories may teach various techniques for curbing anger or managing stress, as well as present alternative behaviors. In using this technique, a brief story—in most cases only five to 10 sentences—is written that shows some of all of the following elements:

- The occurrence of a problem behavior
- The social results of that problem behavior, and/or an alternative behavior or tactic appropriate for the situation
- A strategy for achieving behavioral change
- A reinforcement for changing to more appropriate behavior
- The positive social impact of more appropriate behavior

Why Social Stories Work

As we noted earlier in this chapter, the brain must not only monitor how its owner reacts to external situations when alone, but must also interpret the intentions and responses of others in a social context. Are they friend or foe? Will I learn from them or need to teach them? Do I want their approval or not? Do I care about them? Do they care about me?

These are very complicated notions for a young and immature frontal cortex to process. Jumbled or incomplete processing can lead to inappropriate social responses. Social stories focus the individual's attention on how one's responses affect the behavior of others. An individual's responses, for example, can cause others to accept or reject that individual. Careful construction of the social story can help a student's brain recognize the cause-and-effect nature of social responses. This process may result in more appropriate responses in future social situations.

Preparing Social Stories

Social stories are generally written in the first person in order to emphasize to the students that the social story applies directly to them. Diagrams or line drawings, similar to a comic strip, may be used to create a pictorial representation of the story for students who have difficulty in reading (Jaime & Knowlton, 2007). In other cases, rather than drawings or pictures, actual photographs of the target student may be used in the social story (Haggerty, Black, & Smith, 2005).

An example of a simple comic strip social story for an elementary student is shown in Figure 3.6. In this instance, a student has been talking loudly in the hallway. The teacher has told the student privately that not talking will earn the class two extra minutes of recess. It is important that the

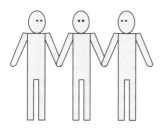

Sometimes we line up in the hallway.

We should be quiet in the hallway so other students can work.

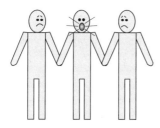

Sometimes I feel like talking loudly, and I begin to talk loudly without thinking about it.

If I remember not to talk, I can earn two minutes of extra recess for the whole class.

The other students smile at me! They like it when I remember not to talk in the hallway.

The teacher likes to give us the extra recess time.

Figure 3.6 This is an example of a social story using comic characters designed to help a student understand that it is important to keep quiet in the hallway.

teacher **not** tell the class that the student's talking will deny them extra recess time as this may cause resentment and rejection. On the other hand, knowing that the student's quiet behavior has **earned** extra recess time may increase the student's acceptance by peers.

A Case Study: Using a Social Story for a Verbally Aggressive Student

Jason's Cursing Behavior

Jason was a second-grade student who often cursed at other students, and this was disruptive in the general education classroom. He had previously been identified as a student with behavioral disorders, and while he was served in a resource room for one period per day, he spent the remainder of his school day in the second grade general education class. The general education teacher, Mr. Anson, consulted with the school psychologist, Ms. Utnay, and they decided to initiate a social story intervention for Jason.

Because most of Jason's misbehavior seemed to occur after lunch, Mr. Anson began a simple count of the occurrences of cursing behavior during that time period each day. He counted each occurrence as one example of cursing, even if Jason used multiple words or sentences in that particular instance. Over a period of five days, it was determined that in the period from the end of lunch until Jason went to the afternoon bus, he cursed at other students an average of 14 times daily. It was also clear that most of Jason's cursing

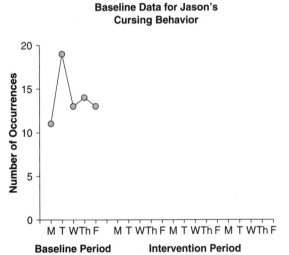

Baseline Data for Jason's Cursing Behavior

Figure 3.7 On this chart, the teacher has recorded the baseline data for Jason's swearing behavior during the week before the intervention.

was impulsive. Some of these instances led to more serious behavior problems and often resulted in fights with other students. The chart in Figure 3.7 shows the baseline data obtained by Mr. Anson. (Note: Throughout this book you will see data collection charts like the one in Figure 3.7. They allow teachers an objective means of determining whether a particular intervention has been successful. See the Appendix for a black-line master of a data chart.)

Creating the Social Story

Starting the Intervention. After baseline data were collected, Mr. Anson and Ms. Utnay began the social story intervention. Ms. Utnay took the lead when the two educators met and talked with

Jason about his cursing behavior. The dialogue below presents part of that initial discussion. Note how the psychologist used the idea of starring in a comic strip to hook Jason into participating.

Ms. Utnay: Jason, Mr. Anson and I wanted to talk with you about an idea we had. Do you remember last week when you had to go to the Principal's office for cursing at Tomika? You got mad at Tomika, and cursed at her during the science lesson. Remember that?

Jason: Yeah, I do.

Ms. Utnay: It wasn't very much fun was it.

Jason: The principal called my Mom, and she kept me from playing outside last Saturday. I was not happy about that, that's for sure!

Ms. Utnay: Well that doesn't sound like much fun at all. Do you remember why you said you cursed at Tomika?

Jason: I just got mad, I guess.

Ms. Utnay: Yes, you told Mr. Anson that you just got mad for no reason and cursed. At other times, you just seem to get mad for no reason, don't you?

Jason: Yeah. I don't know why, but I do.

Ms. Utnay: Well, maybe we can help. Mr. Anson and I have an idea that might help remind you not to curse at other students when you get frustrated. Would you be willing to try something with us?

Jason: What's that?

Ms. Utnay: We want to make a comic strip that can help to remind you not to curse at others. Do you like comic strips?

Jason: Yeah, sure.

Ms. Utnay: Let me tell you the best part. This comic strip will have one star: You! Would you like to star in your own comic strip?

Jason: Yeah! I could show my friends.

Ms. Utnay: You could. You could show your Mom, too, and get her to read it with you. Also, we think it would help to remind you not to curse at others when you get mad. That way you won't get punished.

Jason: OK.

Ms. Utnay: Now to get started, we want to take some pictures of you because you will be the star, and we will need you to act a bit for those pictures. Can you act for those pictures? Can you do that?

Jason: Sure, I can do that. Sounds like fun.

Ms. Utnay: It will be fun. But remember that we are doing this to help you remember not to curse at your friends in the class. That's the important thing here. OK?

Jason: OK.

Preparing the Comic Strip. It was explained to Jason that he would need to pretend for some of the pictures that would be used in the comic strip. In some cases, pictures may be made from actual photos taken during the regular class session, but for pictures involving anger, or severe behaviors, we recommend having the student act out the scene. For Jason's intervention, the sentences shown in Figure 3.8 were prepared as captions for each picture. For older students, these brief sentences may be expanded to three to five sentences for each picture. Note that several appropriate behaviors are suggested as alternatives to the inappropriate behavior of cursing at other students. Also, note the emphasis on the social consequences of Jason's inappropriate behavior.

After the pictures were taken for each sentence in the social story, Jason helped make his own comic strip by pairing the sentences and pictures together. This provided an opportunity for Mr. Anson to discuss these specific feelings and behaviors with Jason, as he prepared the comic strip. In those conversations, Mr. Anson repeatedly stressed that we all sometimes feel anger or

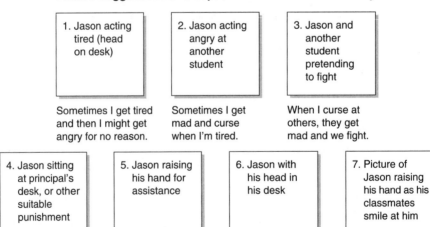

Picture Suggestions and Captions for Jason's Social Story

1. Jason acting tired (head on desk)

Sometimes I get tired and then I might get angry for no reason.

2. Jason acting angry at another student

Sometimes I get mad and curse when I'm tired.

3. Jason and another student pretending to fight

When I curse at others, they get mad and we fight.

4. Jason sitting at principal's desk, or other suitable punishment

When I curse, I sometimes get punished.

5. Jason raising his hand for assistance

Instead of getting mad and cursing, I should ask Mr. Anson for help.

6. Jason with his head in his desk

Another thing I can do when I get angry is to put my head on my desk.

7. Picture of Jason raising his hand as his classmates smile at him

When I chose to do these things instead of cursing, Mr. Anson gives me a sticker and the class is more fun.

Figure 3.8   Here are suggestions for pictures and captions for Jason's social story designed to reduce his cursing behavior.

get our feelings hurt, but that it is important to avoid responding instantly by doing something that leads to punishment. Thus, the very act of preparing for this intervention provides opportunities for Mr. Anson to discuss impulsive behavior with Jason.

Using social stories provides a mechanism for the teacher and student to work together to curb disruptive behavior.

Several distinct elements may be included in a social story, depending upon the needs of the student. One critical factor in creation of the social story is the general order of the caption sentences. They initially identify the behavioral problem and perhaps the feelings that underlie the problem. Next, the positive and negative consequences are presented. In some cases, alternative behaviors might be suggested for the student, as was done in this example, while in other cases, various self-management strategies might be emphasized (see the following example). Note also that the reinforcement for appropriate behavior ("Mr. Anson gives me a sticker!") is emphasized in the social story (Figure 3.8).

Intervening With a Social Story

Once the social story book has been developed, the intervention can proceed. Each day for the next 3 weeks, Mr. Anson read the comic strip to Jason immediately after Jason returned from lunch. This was intended to remind Jason that he should use one of the alternative behaviors rather than cursing at others if he felt himself getting angry. Also, each day after reading the story with Jason, Mr. Anson encouraged Jason to raise his hand when he felt himself getting angry, so that Mr. Anson could walk over to Jason and help him relax. Occasionally, when Mr. Anson saw Jason becoming upset, he would walk over to Jason's desk and ask him quietly if he needed to rest his head for just a minute. In most cases, Jason said yes, and after one minute Mr. Anson could remind him (again, discretely) to lift his head and rejoin the class. One subtle advantage in using social stories is that this tactic makes the teacher an ally of the target student by providing a mechanism for them to work together to curb disruptive behavior.

In some cases when time allowed, after Mr. Anson invited Jason to lift his head, he would also ask Jason to come to the teacher's desk and quietly read the social story together. Again, this offered an opportunity for Mr. Anson to point out that Jason could control his own behavior in a way that did not result in Jason receiving punishment. Those discussions also emphasized the positive alternatives for misbehavior. Finally, at the end of each day during the intervention, Mr. Anson made time to talk briefly with Jason about his behavior. When possible and appropriate, Mr. Anson praised Jason for behavioral improvement and pointed out that he had received many stickers for good work that day.

As can be seen in Figure 3.9, Jason's cursing behavior did decrease significantly over that three-week intervention period. Although cursing was not totally eliminated, it was reduced to a much more

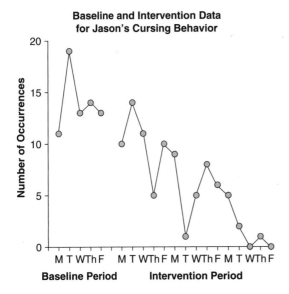

Baseline and Intervention Data for Jason's Cursing Behavior

Figure 3.9 This chart shows the record of Jason's cursing behavior over the three-week period during the intervention. Although the cursing behavior was not eliminated, it was significantly reduced.

manageable level by this intervention. For many students with significant behavior problems, reducing the number of such behaviors, rather than eliminating them altogether, is a much more realistic goal, and does serve to significantly enhance the atmosphere in the general education classroom.

A Social Story for Angry Students

Haggerty, Black, and Smith (2005) reported on a social story intervention that included a component for reducing stress and anger on the part of a six-year-old student with a learning disability. Kirk was described as a student of multiethnic descent who exhibited dyslexia and several other behavioral problems. He functioned in the average range on various IQ assessments, but was angry, inattentive, socially immature, and very anxious.

In implementing the social story tactic for Kirk, the teachers chose to include an emphasis on anger reduction, and they employed a self-statement intervention for that. Thus, this social story actually presented several tactics for self-management of anger. When Kirk felt angry or stressed, he was told to say, "Out with the bad," with each exhale, and "In with the good," with each inhaled breath. This is one form of relaxation that can result in curbing social misbehavior and reducing stress and anger. Kirk's social story book included a total of 8 captions, and given his reading level, the captions were typically several sentences long. Those sentences are shown in Figure 3.10, and in his social story book, each sentence was accompanied by a picture showing Kirk doing the described activity.

In the picture captions, one can see two distinct tactics for curbing impulsive anger ("In with the glad, out with the mad" and "counting to ten" to calm down). Pizzas were counted rather than merely "counting to ten," because inserting the word pizza provided a natural rhythm for that calming process (captions 4, 5, and 6 in Figure 3.10). Thus, Kirk was provided with two strategies for managing his impulsive behavior.

In addition to providing relaxation strategies, this social story also emphasized the social benefits of curbing one's anger (captions 6, 7, and 8 in Figure 3.10). This strategy—perhaps even some version of this same social story—can be used with many angry and defiant students. Teachers seeking new tactics for these challenging kids would do well to consider using this social story intervention.

Picture Suggestions and Captions for Kirk's Social Story

1. Picture shows Kirk angry

Hi! My name is Kirk. Sometimes I get mad. When I get mad, I feel tense. I look like this. I don't like to be mad. So I'm learning how to calm myself.

2. Picture shows Kirk breathing in

When I feel tense, I calm myself by breathing in deeply. Then I say, "In with the glad." It feels good when I do this. I like doing this. My teachers and friends like it, too.

3. Picture shows Kirk breathing out

The next thing I do is breathe out and say, "Out with the mad." I push the mad out. This is fun. I like doing this. I do this three times. It makes me feel less tense.

4. Picture shows four slices of pizza, numbered 1 through 4

Then I count to ten pizzas. I start with 1 pizza, 2 pizzas, 3 pizzas, 4 pizzas. This is fun. I feel better already.

5. Picture shows five slices of pizza, numbered 5 through 9

Then 5 pizzas, 6 pizzas, 7 pizzas, 8 pizzas, 9 pizzas. Wow! I feel good.

6. Picture shows Kirk smiling and holding up 10 fingers

Ten pizzas. Yes, I did it! I feel so good. I am happy and my teacher is happy. My friends are happy, too. I like feeling this way. I like feeling calm.

7. Picture shows Kirk smiling

I'm glad I learned to stop being mad. I feel so calm. I feel happy. I like taking care of myself. My teachers and friends like it, too.

8. Picture shows Kirk and teacher sitting, smiling; teacher's arm around Kirk

My teacher is very proud of me. She says I stop being mad very well. She tells my friends what a good job I do. I like my new skill.

Figure 3.10   These are picture and caption suggestions for Kirk's social story to reduce his stress and anger.

43

Guidelines for Developing Social Stories

The following are additional points that teachers should consider when developing a social story intervention (Agosta, Graetz, Mastropieri, & Scruggs, 2004; Jaime & Knowlton, 2007).

- **Write in the Third Person.** Writing the social story in the first person may make the story too intimate for some shy students. For those students, some researchers have recommended writing the social story in the third person.
- **Use the Present Tense.** Use verbs in the present tense in the social story because this makes the problem and the solutions seem more immediate to the student.
- **Emphasize the Positive.** The captions in the social stories generally emphasize what students should do and not what they should not do.
- **Maintain Respect.** The captions always use language that is respectful of all students and, in particular, the student with the behavioral problem. Stressing the distinction between the student and the misbehavior is critical, and the social stories give students the sense that they can control their own behavior.

Effectiveness of Social Stories

The social stories intervention has been successfully used with different types of students who display various behavioral problems, and research has repeatedly demonstrated the effectiveness of this intervention. Most of the research has been conducted using students with autism as subjects (Agosta et al., 2004; Parsons, 2006). However, other research has implemented this tactic for students with Asperger Syndrome (Rogers & Myles, 2001) or students with dyslexia and oppositional behavior (Haggerty, Black, & Smith, 2005). Further, this research has shown social stories to be effective for students in the primary grades through high school.

Notice in the previous examples of the social stories interventions the continuing emphasis on relationships with both teachers and students. The importance of these relationships for most students provides a potent basis for this intervention. Even students who say and act as if they do not care what their peers or teachers think, often really do care. Using these relationships as a hook to involve students in interventions to curb their own behavioral problems can be beneficial and productive (Stipek, 2006).

One caution is in order. Older students with more mild disabilities, such as learning disabilities or mild behavioral problems, may find this comic strip tactic to be juvenile, and thus may not wish to participate. However, others across the school age range may enjoy having a social story book made about them. Like all strategies, the teacher determines the student's general maturity and interest in participation prior to implementing this tactic.

There are several sources of social stories on the Internet, such as the Gray Center for Social Learning and Understanding. See the **Resources** section for more information about this center.

SUMMARY

Social behavior is greatly influenced by how the brain develops and organizes and interprets information from its environment. Emotional responses to one's environment are normal and their excesses are kept under control by the brain's executive control system. But given its strong genetic directive to keep its owner alive, the immature brain can sometimes misinterpret harmless social situations as threatening and overreact with an inappropriate response. If there are few or no consequences resulting from this misbehavior, then it is likely to continue. Faced with this situation, there are some interventions, such as social stories and others, that teachers can use to effectively moderate social misbehavior.

Addressing Students Who Cause Class Disruptions

4

Kay Burke

Figure 4.0   Phases of a Power Struggle Explosion

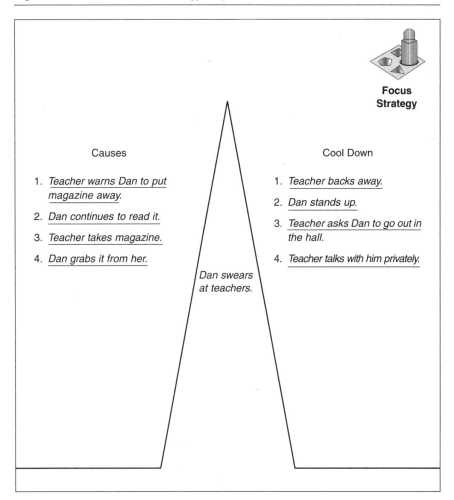

Focus Strategy

Causes

1. *Teacher warns Dan to put magazine away.*
2. *Dan continues to read it.*
3. *Teacher takes magazine.*
4. *Dan grabs it from her.*

Dan swears at teachers.

Cool Down

1. *Teacher backs away.*
2. *Dan stands up.*
3. *Teacher asks Dan to go out in the hall.*
4. *Teacher talks with him privately.*

ADDRESSING BEHAVIOR PROBLEMS

When students display inappropriate behavior, they do so because they have the **mistaken goal** *that it will get them the recognition and acceptance they want.* (Dreikers, Grunwald, & Pepper as cited in Vaughn, Bos, & Schumm, 2000, p. 81)

Behavior problems constitute student behaviors that cause disruptions in the class. Such behaviors can be directed at other students or the teacher and may include talking when another student or the teacher is talking, name calling, fighting, arguing, throwing things, or getting up out of one's seat. Although any of these behaviors is enough to disrupt a classroom, most of them can be controlled by a proactive teacher.

Curwin and Mendler (1988) propose the 80-15-5 model, in which they estimate that 80 percent of students in most classes never or rarely break the classroom rules and cause disruptions. They estimate that about 15 percent of students break rules on a regular basis and 5 percent are chronic rule breakers. Walsh (as cited in Levin & Nolan, 1996) reports that some teachers spend as much as 30 to 80 percent of their time addressing discipline problems. It is evident that the successful teacher of the twenty-first century needs to be able to manage students to maximize the time spent on learning. With the increased emphasis on high-stakes standardized tests, standards, and accountability, teachers must increase time-on-task to prepare students to meet rigorous academic goals.

Most children lack the skills to handle the conflict situations they face. DeRoche and Williams (2001) say these skills include communication skills (listening and verbal/nonverbal messages), problem-solving skills (identifying problems, brainstorming solutions, finding win-win solutions), and cooperative skills (working collaboratively to complete tasks). They say that

these conflict resolution skills should be taught to students through situations that allow them to practice using the skills in realistic contexts. Students need frequent guided practice in these skills to make them feel comfortable enough to use them to resolve conflicts when they arise. (p. 30)

Because many students lack these conflict resolution skills, they sometimes resort to the only methods they know to try to solve conflicts. Often their methods involve inappropriate behaviors.

Ripple Effect

Teachers are concerned not only with addressing student disruptions but also with the "ripple effect" (Kounin as cited in Levin & Nolan, 1996). The ripple effect results from the initial misbehavior, the methods the teacher uses to curb the misbehavior, and the resultant behavior of the targeted student.

Studies have shown that rough and threatening teacher behavior causes student anxieties, which lead to additional disruptive behaviors from on-looking students. However, students who see that disruptive students comply with the teacher's control technique rate their teacher as fairer and are themselves less distracted from their classwork than when they observe unruly students defying the teacher." (Smith as cited in Levin & Nolan, p. 29)

Many complex dynamics come into play when a teacher addresses even a minor behavior disruption.

At-Risk Students

Educators often use the term *at risk* to describe a particular category of students. A profile of at-risk students has evolved that helps educators make predictions regarding a student's self-concept, behavior, and educational needs. Barr and Parrett (2003) say this profile often describes the

low socioeconomic students living in homes of poverty, often with only a single parent, grandparent, or a foster parent. These students, often identified prior to arriving at school through interactions with social agencies or identified through free and reduced lunch program applications, often constitute a significant percentage of the school's enrollment. (p. 39)

Poverty

Educators need to learn more about how these students live to anticipate their behavioral and academic needs. These students can achieve both social and academic success, but they may need more help.

Payne (as cited in Tileston, 2004) defines poverty as being more than just money. She says poverty is the extent to which an individual does without resources. She defines resources as the following:

- Financial—Money to purchase goods
- Emotional—Ability to respond appropriately to situations and having the role models to demonstrate this
- Mental—The mental abilities and skills needed in daily life
- Spiritual—Belief in a divine purpose and guidance
- Physical—Good health
- Support systems—Friends and family and backup resources in times of need
- Role models—Frequent and appropriate role models who are adults
- Knowledge of hidden rules (p. 71)

Moreover, children who are poor may be at greater risk of failing their classes, dropping out of school before graduation, and turning violent.

The added pressure on these at-risk students to meet high academic standards under the No Child Left Behind Act compounds their problems. Rothstein, a research associate at the Economic Policy Institute, is concerned that students from all demographic groups must meet high academic standards without regard to their poverty, substandard housing, and inadequate health care. In his 2004 book, *Class and Schools,* he writes, "the influence of social class characteristics is probably so powerful that schools cannot overcome it, no matter how well-trained are their teachers and no matter how well-designed are their instructional programs and climates (as cited in Holland, 2007, p. 54).

Labeling students is a challenge because at-risk conditions are not clear-cut and what causes one student to be at risk may not affect other students the same way. Short, Short, and Blanton (1994) discuss how students who are low achievers in school activities are described as at-risk students. Some of the characteristics they describe for an at-risk child include not having mastered basic skills, having been retained, being below grade level on test scores, having a poor attendance record, having a record of suspensions, qualifying for free or reduced lunch, or having a history of high mobility. In addition, at-risk students could have experienced child abuse or neglect; abused substances; have experienced racial, cultural, or gender bias; or come from a dysfunctional family. "A large proportion of school-age children either are or will be poor, multicultural/minority, and from nontraditional homes— all characteristics that have been related to school and social failure" (p. 75).

Even though the characteristics of at-risk students are mostly extrinsic to the child, they still have a profound effect on the development and performance of the student in school. Moreover, at-risk students often display characteristics that distinguish them from the rest of their peer group. This difference can cause tremendous social pressures that result in their not fitting in with the social structure of the class and exhibiting recurrent discipline problems in school (Short et al., 1994).

Teachers have to be aware of the "baggage" many students bring to school each day. They need to be as fair and consistent as possible in maintaining high expectations for all students and enforcing classroom procedures, rules, and consequences. They must also, however, be aware of students' situations and the philosophical idea that "fair is not always equal." Moreover, each student should be handled with some consideration, respect, and flexibility, if possible. Kati Haycock, the director of Education Trust, believes that skilled and dedicated educators can succeed with disadvantaged children and close the achievement gap if they provide rich curricula and quality instruction. "There is no question when you look at both research and our experience around the country that expert teachers are the heart of any solution" (Haycock as cited in Holland, 2007, p. 57).

Identifying Antecedents

The events or conditions that immediately precede instances of problem behavior are called antecedents (Kauffman, Hallahan, Mostert, Trent, & Nuttycombe, 1993). Teachers can keep an anecdotal record or written notes to describe a pattern of when, where, and under what conditions the behavior most often occurs.

For example, if Jimmy usually becomes rude and obnoxious right before a major test, the teacher might have a private conference with him to find out why. Maybe he can't read the directions or he feels inadequate. Maybe he can't handle the time constraints of a test and would like more time. Maybe he can't understand the multiple-choice format and would do better on a performance task that demonstrates what he actually knows rather than how well he guesses.

Effective teachers look for patterns to identify specific events, times of the day, or activities that cause students to act out. One event that often causes disruptions is assigning students to groups. If Kathy hates Jenny because of a problem with an old boyfriend, she may cause a disruption to avoid working with Jenny on a cooperative project. Obviously, teachers cannot anticipate every potential problem, but the proactive teacher can diffuse potential problems before they become major disruptions.

Coercive Interaction

Kauffman et al. (1993) discuss the typical situations that occur when a pupil finds a teacher's expectations and demands aversive or unpleasant. The teacher, in turn, finds the student's refusal to follow his order also aversive and, therefore, restates the demand and adds a threat or punishment as an "incentive." The student then feels challenged in front of her peer group and becomes even louder, more obnoxious, and more threatened, causing the teacher to respond with more severe threats of punishment. This type of coercive interaction continues until the teacher "wins" and the student backs down. This retreat is sometimes temporary, lasting only until the student seeks revenge on the teacher for "beating" her in public. Another typical situation results in the teacher's backing down and not following through with the threat, in which case the student wins. In this case, sometimes the teacher is "out to get the student" the rest of the year because he lost face in front of the class. The best situation is a win-win outcome where both parties compromise, save face, and address the real cause of the problem and possible solutions in private.

Figure 4.1 represents a typical coercive classroom interaction. Skillful teachers can avoid such coercive interactions and recognize when students are baiting them to seek attention or engage in a power struggle.

Figure 4.1   Coercive Interaction

- Teacher asks student to complete page of math problems.
- Student says, "I don't know how to do this crap!"
- Teacher says, "Yes you do, we just did some problems like these yesterday. Get started now."
- Student slams book closed, saying, "Ain't doin' it!"
- Teacher goes to student's desk, opens book, hands student pencil, says in angry tone, "Get started now!"
- Student shoves book off desk.
- Teacher squeezes student's shoulder, growls, "Pick that book up, young man!"
- Student jumps to feet, says, "Get your hands off me, b———— ! You pick it up! You can't make me do nothin'!"
- Teacher yells, "That's it! I've had enough of this! Pick that book up and get to work now or you're outta here to the office!"

STUDENTS WHO SEEK ATTENTION

Scenario

Glenn gets up from his desk, slowly walks down the aisle to the pencil sharpener, and starts sharpening a long pencil. Each time he finishes sharpening, he puts the pencil inside the sharpener again and again until it becomes a stub.

"Sit down," yells Mrs. Martinez. "We're trying to work here, and you're not supposed to be out of your desk."

"I'm just trying to sharpen my pencil," Glenn announces loudly to the entire class. "Is that a crime? Excuse me for living!"

Mrs. Martinez walks over to Glenn and whispers quietly, "Glenn, the class is working on their group art project, and your group really needs your help."

Glenn reluctantly rejoins his group and proceeds to draw a happy face on the back of Mary's black sweater with a piece of hot-pink colored chalk.

"You idiot," shrieks Mary. "When are you going to grow up?"

Glenn laughs and looks around the room to see all the students and Mrs. Martinez staring at him.

Mrs. Martinez walks over and taps Glenn on the shoulder, and they both walk into the hall.

Solving the Problem

Misbehaving students are often seeking *extra* attention. Albert (1989) says that all people need a certain amount of attention to feel as though they belong and are an important part of the social group. "In contrast, students who misbehave for attention are never satisfied with a normal amount. They want more and more, as if they carry around with them a bucket labeled 'attention' that they expect the teacher to fill" (p. 26).

Attention seekers are students who seek independence but spend a great deal of their time complaining to others that they cannot control what is happening in their lives. "They see themselves as victims of circumstance and strive to gain attention by keeping adults busy with them" (Dinkmeyer, McKay, & Dinkmeyer, 1980, p. 252).

Many attention seekers are discouraged students who may become obnoxiously loud and silly or resort to immature acts, like pushing books off a desk or trying to trip someone, to get noticed. Attention seekers are like stage performers; they require an audience. They do get noticed, but many of them eventually get rejected by their peers and their teacher, who grow tired of their constant attempts to be in the limelight. The attention seeker's idea of success is to be on stage, even if their actions violate the dignity and rights of other students and earn her the hostility of those who feel attacked or violated (Dinkmeyer & Losoncy, 1980). In the elementary grades, attention seekers usually gear their performance toward the teacher, but as they move to upper grades, they prefer a wider audience that includes their classmates, guidance counselors, administrators, and sometimes the entire school community (Albert, 1989).

Appropriate Attention

The origins of attention-seeking behavior range from students' not receiving enough attention at home to students' not knowing how to ask for attention in an appropriate manner. The greatest challenge for teachers is to change the behavior of the attention seeker by giving him as little attention as possible when the misbehavior occurs. Bellanca and Fogarty (2003) recommend the following strategies:

- Highlight other students who are behaving appropriately.
- Move the student out of the spotlight by giving him an errand to run.
- Distract the student with a question.
- Attend to the attention seeker positively when she is on task.

By encouraging attention seekers to succeed in individual or group work and by noticing and encouraging their accomplishments, teachers and students reinforce appropriate behavior with positive attention. The goal is to encourage attention seekers to strive for positive attention, rather than negative attention, from peers and teachers to fulfill their needs.

Because one method to prevent students from seeking attention is to identify the goal of the misbehavior, teachers should help students to analyze their own behavior. The Newspaper Model (see Figure 4.2) allows attention seekers to analyze their actions and reflect on the causes and effects of their behavior. Figure 4.3 offers a Newspaper Model template that teachers can use with their students. Teachers should work with students to fill out the form and discuss and reflect on the process.

Educators must remember that the number of students seeking attention will probably increase commensurate with the lack of attention they may be getting from their families at home. Large class sizes and big schools can cause many students to feel lost in the crowd. Some larger secondary schools have adopted the "school within a school" structure or Freshmen Academies to provide smaller learning communities, so students feel more connected to their peer group and teachers. When students have to compete for attention each day, they may resort to more disruptive or even violent ways to capture the attention of their parents, teachers, and classmates—even the media.

Other Strategies Teachers Can Use With Students Who Seek Attention

- Help the student find an area where she can shine. Find a specific interest or strength she can use to get attention in a positive way.
- Find the student a study buddy. Sometimes a student who lacks friends tries to compensate by acting out.

Figure 4.2 The Newspaper Model

Ask the student to describe the problem by writing down who was involved, what happened, when the problem occurred, where the problem occurred, and why it happened. Then the attention seeker should write a paragraph about the situation and share the paragraph with others involved in the problem.

Focus Strategy

Name: _____Glenn_____   Date: ___Feb. 3_____

Problem: _____I got in trouble for sharpening my pencil and drawing on Mary's sweater_____

Who	What	When	Where	Why
(me) Glenn	Caused a disturbance by sharpening my pencil and drawing on Mary's sweater	Tuesday Feb. 3 during 5th period	In Mrs. Martinez's art class at Oak School	Because I was mad that the teacher and Mary had yelled at me

Write a paragraph describing your view of what happened.

I got mad because John and Mary think they are better than me. They never use my ideas when we meet in groups. They are always calling me names and putting me down. I went to sharpen my pencil to get away from the group. Then I got mad when Mary laughed when I got in trouble. I showed the class who got the last laugh.

Signed: _____Glenn_____

Have another group member write a paragraph about the situation.

I called Glenn a jerk because he is always fooling around instead of helping. I know I shouldn't call him names, but I get really frustrated with him. I laughed at him when Mrs. Martinez yelled at him because I told him not to do it. I get very angry at him.

Signed: _____Mary_____

Figure 4.3   The Newspaper Model Template

Name: _____   Date: _____
Problem: _____

Who	What	When	Where	Why

Write a paragraph describing your view of what happened.

Signed: _____

Have another group member write a paragraph about the situation.

Signed: _____

- Give the student an option of a short time-out period. He can go to a corner of the room to cool down or write in a journal about his feelings.
- Analyze the Newspaper Model to see when, where, and why most incidents occur. Remember to review the antecedents or context. If incidents usually arise from the student's being involved with certain people or situations, try to avoid placing the student in those situations.
- When a student does something well, encourage her.
- When a student raises his hand, call on him quickly to give him positive attention for an answer or for trying to answer a question.
- Give the student legitimate positive attention by allowing her to go to the Media Center, lead the "Pledge of Allegiance," or conduct an Internet search. Be careful to rotate these privileges regularly so the other students don't resent her.
- Have a secret signal to give the student from across the room to remind him when he is doing something to get attention.

Add some of your own solutions for helping students who seek attention:

_____

_____

_____

_____

_____

STUDENTS WHO SEEK POWER

Scenario

Mrs. Bradley returns the students' English tests and then asks if there are any questions.
"This sucks!" exclaims Brian. "You can't take off points for misspellings. We weren't allowed to use dictionaries!"
"You should know how to spell the words you write. I take off five points for every error."
"You can't do that!" Brian yells, moving forward in his desk. "This test was on short stories, and we were supposed to describe the plots. Who cares if we misspelled a few words. You missed the point of the test! We didn't get to use spell check!"
"Excuse me, young man," Mrs. Bradley snarls as her face turns red. "This is my class, and I will be the one who decides what I will and will not grade!"
"This sucks," mutters Brian. "I want to go to my counselor to get transferred to Mrs. Brown's English class."
"You're not getting a pass from me," counters Mrs. Bradley.
"I don't need a pass—I'm outta here." Brian grabs his backpack and kicks his desk before he bolts from the room.
The other students glare at Mrs. Bradley in silence.

Solving the Problem

"I believe that the need for power is the core—the absolute core—of almost all school problems" (Glasser as cited in Gough, 1987, p. 658).

Students who seek independence sometimes engage in power conflicts with adults because they are determined not to do what adults want. Curwin and Mendler (1988) warn teachers not to get caught in a power trap:

> Commit yourself to avoiding power struggles, even if it means initially backing down. Remember that continuation of a power struggle makes you look foolish and out of control. You must be prepared to see long-term victory (a cooperative, positive classroom climate) as more important than short-term winning. (p. 105)

Glasser (1986) feels that students, even good students, don't feel important in school because no one listens to them. Moreover, students who receive poor grades and are considered discipline problems cannot feel important from the standpoint of academic performance·and acceptance. Glasser asserts that students would work harder in school if they had more freedom and fun. Mendler (1997) says, "It is estimated that 70 to 80 percent of challenging student behavior in school is primarily attributable to outside factors such as dysfunctional families, violence in our culture, the effects of drugs and alcohol, and fragmented communities" (p. 4). Yet teachers cannot relinquish their responsibility for controlling student behavior in their classrooms by blaming it on outside forces. The challenge is to teach all students.

Most often, the power base in schools is tilted in favor of teachers. Teachers have the power to threaten students and can back up those threats with minus points, minutes in the time-out area, detention, notes to parents, suspensions, expulsion, and the ultimate weapon—failure. Despite all the power teachers have, Glasser (1986) says that half the students still won't work because they don't feel they have any control over their lives. They are discouraged because they have so little to say about what they learn, when they learn it, and how they learn it. Students are discouraged, and they don't have the patience to wait it out until teachers and the school system give them more say in their education. Power seekers vent this frustration through temper tantrums, verbal tantrums, and quiet noncompliance (Albert, 1989).

More and more schools recognize the need to empower students by allowing them to be involved in setting classroom rules and having some choice in what they study and how they will be assessed.

> Students also need to learn to look for more effective behaviors while they wait, but they have less power over their lives than adults and little confidence that the school will change for the better. If we can restructure schools so that they are more satisfying, we can expect many more students to be patient when they are frustrated. (Glasser, 1986, p. 55)

The tactics in Figure 4.4 can be used by teachers to avoid getting pulled into a power struggle.

Figure 4.4   Tactics Teachers Can Use With Power Seekers

- Don't grab the hook. Teachers should not fall into the power trap, especially in front of the class.
- Avoid and defuse direct confrontations.
- Listen to the problem in private.
- Recognize the student's feelings.
- Privately acknowledge the power struggle.
- Do not embarrass students publicly.
- Give the students choices in their academic work.
- Place the power seeker in a leadership role.
- Encourage independent thinking—but not anarchy!

Students who seek power often try to dominate the entire class and their groups. If they cannot control the class, the teacher, or the school, they might consider their cooperative group as their personal power base. Teachers should monitor the roles assigned to group members and make sure that power seekers are fulfilling their assignments without trying to take control of the entire group.

Teachers should also review the specific roles assigned to each group member and the responsibilities of each of these roles every time they assign cooperative group work. Remind students that group roles are rotated so everyone will have a chance to be the organizer or the group leader. If the tasks are structured so that they allow a great deal of choice, creativity, and freedom, power seekers should be satisfied that they do, in fact, have some control over their lives. Hopefully, they will develop positive leadership qualities rather than negative dictatorial traits. Figure 4.5 shows the phases in a power struggle.

The most difficult behavior for teachers to model when engaged in a power struggle with a student is self-control. Jones and Jones (2001) warn teachers to guard against their vulnerabilities and be "smarter than a trout." They warn, "Like the wily trout who knows better than to strike at every imitation lure, we

Figure 4.5

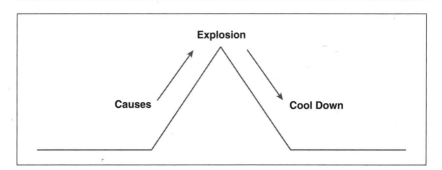

must be careful not to become snared by students' attempts to gain control or negative attention by making inappropriate comments" (p. 309).

Teachers need to be proactively aware of when students become upset, look angry or frustrated, depressed or anxious. If teachers practice their best "with-it-ness" strategies, they will be able to select the most appropriate option to deescalate the behavior thoughtfully and purposefully.

Figure 4.6 shows how the student and the teacher in this scenario can use Phases of a Power Struggle to analyze what they could have done differently to prevent a power struggle. Figure 4.7 is a Phases of a Power Struggle Template that teachers can use with their own students. The graphic organizer and strategy developed by Bob Wiedmann shows the initial causes that escalate the problem, the explosion, and the cooldown phases of a power struggle. This graphic organizer helps both the teacher and the student analyze the "hot points" or "key words and actions" that cause a minor comment or incident to escalate into a full-scale power struggle from which neither the teacher nor the student emerges victorious.

Power-seeking students constantly challenge teachers by trying to prove they are in control of issues such as tardiness, incomplete work, making noises, gum chewing, or muttering under their breath. Albert (1989) reminds teachers,

> Often power-seeking students don't act out until they're assured of an audience. We fear that if we lose a public battle, we'll be labeled a "loser" by the entire class until school is out in June. The pressure of having to handle such a difficult situation with so much at stake in front of an audience adds greatly to our discomfort. (p. 44)

Urban Teaching

Weiner (1999) discusses how young teachers going into urban schools, who have not lived in the communities their school serves, can be more anxious about managing their classrooms. Because a great many kids from poor neighborhoods are surrounded by violence, they develop a "defensive stance" and aggressive behavior as survival mechanisms. If urban schools don't adequately safeguard students and their property, students might ignore classroom rules because they feel vulnerable. They might reject the school's behavioral norms because they don't feel the rules protect them enough. "Children often violate school rules of conduct, sacrificing their prospect of academic success to safeguard themselves and their belonging because they do not trust authorities in schools to provide them with adequate protection" (Weiner, p. 68).

Teachers need to ensure that their classrooms are safe and orderly and that the property of the students is secure. If the environment is safe, students will be more inclined to follow rules and principles and refrain from engaging in power struggles to maintain their pride and guarantee their own safety.

Some students are more resilient and are capable of accepting change and recovering more quickly from problems and adversities. Gholar and Riggs (2004) describe resilient teachers and students who are able to demonstrate flexibility, optimism, endurance, and an openness to learn. They believe that conative intelligence (CI) builds upon "the winner within" to help students love learning and raise their performance in significant ways. They describe conative

Figure 4.6 Phases of a Power Struggle

The teacher and the student involved in an altercation should fill out the form to find out what they did to provoke the struggle and what they can do in the future to prevent or resolve the problem.

Focus Strategy

Explosion

Causes

1. *Mrs. Bradley deducted points for spelling errors.*
2. *Brian swore at her.*
3. *Mrs. Bradley yelled at Brian.*

Brian defies Mrs. Bradley and storms out of the class.

Cool down

1. *Mrs. Bradley calms down and returns to the next lesson.*
2. *Brian meets with his counselor.*
3. *The counselor schedules a meeting with both them.*

What the teacher could have done to prevent the problem:
I should have told the students my criteria for grading before the test. I should have taken Brian out in the hall when he blew up.

What the student could have done to prevent the problem:
I should have asked to speak to Mrs. Bradley after class in private. I should not have lost my temper in class.

Resolution to problem:
Both Mrs. Bradley and Brian will talk to the class. Mrs. Bradley will promise to share her grading procedures prior to the tests in the future. Brian will apologize for his language and behavior. He will serve two detentions for violating school policy. Both will make an effort to conduct all disagreements in private—not in front of the class.

Teacher: *Mrs. Bradley*   Student: *Brian*   Date: *Oct. 4*

Figure 4.7   Phases of a Power Struggle Template

Explosion

Causes

1. _____
   _____
2. _____
   _____
3. _____
   _____

Cool down

1. _____
   _____
2. _____
   _____
3. _____
   _____

What the teacher could have done to prevent the problem:

What the student could have done to prevent the problem:

Resolution to problem:

Teacher: _____   Student: _____   Date:_____

intelligence as "the ability to persist, pursue, strive, and commit to a goal; understand the role of persistence in high performance; and productively engage the energy of the will in active teaching and learning" (p. 18). When people utilize their conative intelligence, they strive to make wise choices, and they pursue personal and academic goals. Students who don't have this inner confidence to succeed might engage in power struggles with their peers, parents, and teachers to hide their feelings of insecurity or sense of powerlessness.

Teachers who are able to instill the power of positive thinking in students can change students' views of themselves and the world around them.

Other Strategies Teachers Can Use With Students Who Seek Power

- Keep cool and remain calm. The power-seeking student often tries to excite and anger the teacher and fellow students.
- Isolate the student from other group members or classmates. Don't allow a confrontation to erupt where people say and do things they later regret.
- Allow the student some time to cool down and get herself together. Let her go to a private area (office, media center, counselor, time-out corner) so she can compose herself.
- Defuse his anger by saying, "I see your point," or, "I know how you must feel," but then state what you think is necessary.
- Delay the issue by saying, "You can stay in your seat now, and I'll consider giving you a pass later."
- Conference with the student to find out if any personal or family problems are making her anxious or belligerent. Sometimes the blow-up is not caused by the minor incident that precipitated it; it is because of personal problems.
- Write a contract with the student to brainstorm alternative ideas he might try when he is upset and wants to take control of the class or the group.
- Try to give her a leadership position in one of the next class activities. She can then exercise her leadership role in a positive, rather than negative, way.
- Reinforce anything the student does that is positive. Encourage his actions when he maintains his cool.
- Have the student keep a "Power Problem Journal" to record the specific things that upset her. The student will get time to process her feelings and reflect on her behavior. Self-analysis is a powerful tool in redirecting behavior.

Add some of your own solutions for helping students who seek power:

_____

_____

_____

_____

_____

STUDENTS WHO SEEK REVENGE

Scenario

> Coach Carden passes out the history test papers and proceeds to lecture the class.
>
> "You must not care about passing this class and getting into college. These tests are pathetic! Did anyone here bother reading the chapter on the Civil War?" he asks sarcastically.
>
> Rick stares at his 62 percent score and doesn't say a word. Then he suddenly crumbles his paper into a ball and tosses it toward the garbage can. It misses!
>
> "Some basketball player you are," scoffs Coach Carden. "I'm glad I'm not your coach."
>
> "I might not be a basketball player after I get my grade for this class. This sucks!" yells Rick.
>
> "What did you say? You know I don't tolerate that kind of language in this class. See me after school today for an hour detention. We'll practice how to carry on a polite conversation."
>
> "You can go to hell!" Rick shouts. "I have practice after school. You can't make me stay."
>
> "Oh yeah, we'll see about that. You'll stay or you'll be suspended and miss a few games!" replies Coach Carden.
>
> "That's not fair. You can't flunk the whole class and you can't make me stay in this sorry excuse for a class. I'm out of here."
>
> Rick storms out of the room shouting, "We'll see what my parents and my coach say when they hear about this. My dad's a lawyer! I'll see you in court!"

Solving the Problem

Sometimes power seekers who never satisfy their need for power become revenge seekers to get back at the person or persons who thwarted their quest for power. Usually the revengeful student is trying to retaliate for something hurtful said by a parent, teacher, or peer or for some injustice or unfair deed. Albert (1989) says these students often sulk or scowl even when not lashing out. They put teachers on edge because teachers are never sure when these students will retaliate.

The most important thing teachers can do for students who are seeking revenge is to help them rebuild positive relationships with the teacher or the class. It may be difficult for a teacher to build a caring relationship with someone who has just announced to the whole class that the teacher "sucks," but it is important. The social skill of encouragement needs to be emphasized, and teachers should monitor group activities to make sure the revenge seeker is included. The student who seeks revenge needs to learn appropriate methods to express his hurt or anger appropriately by talking to the teacher or to peers to resolve the problem. Teachers themselves can try come of the tactics shown in Figure 4.8 with revenge seekers to encourage positive behavior and to reduce power struggles.

Revenge seekers need to have their desire to "get even" defused, or else their hidden agenda may torpedo the class. When this happens, the other students may become resentful and distrustful of the revenge seeker. As a result, the revenge seeker compounds her personal problems by alienating her peers in addition to the teacher whom she is out to get.

The revenge seeker's hidden agenda can snowball into a personality problem that serves to brand the student as a "bully," "incorrigible," or a "loner" for the rest of the year or even the rest of his schooling. Teachers need to take time

Figure 4.8   Tactics Teachers Can Use With Revenge Seekers

- Avoid sarcasm or put-downs.
- Do not confront the student in front of her peers.
- Don't seek revenge on revenge seekers.
- Listen carefully to his problems (probe for causes).
- Form a positive relationship with the student.
- Encourage the student when she behaves appropriately.
- Ask the student to keep a journal to process feelings and analyze the causes for his anger.
- Admit mistakes.
- Use frequent teacher-student conferences to monitor behavior.

from the textbook and curriculum to allow students to process their emotions. Conference with the student, call in a counselor or another teacher to talk to the student, have the student keep a diary or journal to record events that trigger an outburst, and analyze different responses.

If students are not happy, satisfied, and accepted in the classroom, they will continue to disrupt learning and interfere with group interactions until their personal needs are met—sometimes at a very extreme level. For example, the violence across American schools, especially in Columbine, Colorado, in 1999 and on the Virginia Tech Campus in 2007, can be linked to students who were enraged. When enraged students kill, they are often trying to extort revenge on those whom they perceived disrespected them. Sometimes, however, the violence is more random, and the enraged student seeks revenge on anyone in his path. There is a strong link between student revenge seekers and school violence.

The Divided Journal (see Figure 4.9) allows both teachers and students to reflect on what they may have said or done in anger and propose another way they could approach the problem if it occurs again. Sometimes these journals help teachers learn more about the inappropriateness of their own actions and how their behavior escalated a minor incident into a showdown. The ultimate revenge of a teacher is failing the student, but students should not suffer academically for their poor behavior. The problem needs to be addressed so it doesn't distract from learning.

The Divided Journal allows both teachers and students to reflect metacognitively on their actions. Given (2002) says that the Russian psychologist A. R. Luria described the use of "self-talk" to regulate one's behavior. Luria observed that prefrontal cortical damage often created impulsive behavior, explosive anger, and fear. He also found that students could be taught to use self-talk to curb their impulsive acts and function appropriately. The reflective system allows people to carry on dialogues in their heads, try out ideas, rethink interactions, and project the results of an action without actually doing it. Given says, "This allows us to cultivate thinking strategies and attitudes we can use to control genetic predispositions" (p. 121). In other words, students can self-monitor and manage their behavior through reflective learning. The journal is a metacognitive tool for students and teachers to *analyze* their thoughts and behavior and then act to attain their goals.

Figure 4.9   Divided Journal

The teacher and the student need to process what happened by describing the incident and reflecting on what they would do differently. They should discuss their reactions and try to arrive at a mutually beneficial compromise.

Focus Strategy

Student: _____Rick_____ Date: _____April 5_____

Description of What Happened

I was angry because I'd studied hard for the test and Coach was yelling about how we weren't going to get into college.

I freaked out and threw my test away. It upset him, but I was upset that I might get kicked off the basketball team. Basketball means everything to me.

Upon Reflection   Date: _____April 6_____

What I Would Do Differently

I realize that Coach was trying to motivate us to study harder. I should have talked to him after class about what I could do to bring up my grade. Then I would have been calmer and wouldn't have tried to save face with the class. I should never have threatened him with a lawsuit!

Teacher: _____Coach Carden_____ Date: _____April 5_____

Description of What Happened

I passed out the tests and talked to the class about their poor performance. Rick was upset and threw his test away.

I was upset because I had planned to review the test and discuss the right answers. He tried to get back at me in front of the class.

Upon Reflection   Date: _____April 6_____

What I Would Do Differently

I should not have passed out the test that way because kids saw each other's papers. I think Rick was embarrassed because one of the cheerleaders saw his 62 percent.

I shouldn't have made fun of him when he missed the trash with his wadded-up test. I hurt him, and he reacted the only way he could—to save face with his peers.

Figure 4.10 offers a Divided Journal template that teachers can use with their students. Reflection is a powerful tool to help adults, teenagers, and even young children process their feelings and analyze their actions in private.

Figure 4.10 Divided Journal Template

Student: _____ Date: _____	Upon Reflection Date: _____
Description of What Happened	**What I Would Do Differently**
Teacher: _____ Date: _____	Upon Reflection Date: _____
Description of What Happened	**What I Would Do Differently**

Other Strategies Teachers Can Use
With Students Who Seek Revenge

- Use I-messages: "When I see you losing your temper, I feel upset because . . . "
- Ask for a conference with the student and ask to have a counselor present as an objective observer.
- Encourage students who have questions or concerns about assignments or grades to see you privately after class.
- Build in some downtime during class, while students are working, when you are available to discuss problems (especially for students who cannot come in after school).
- Fold over test papers and return them personally to students to preserve confidentiality.
- Don't take the hook. Teenagers are often not in control of their emotions, but teachers should try to be in control of their emotions.

Add some of your own solutions for helping students who seek revenge:

_____

_____

_____

_____

_____

STUDENTS WITH AGGRESSIVE BEHAVIORS

Scenario

Ms. Cox divides the class into cooperative groups and posts the directions for their projects on the board.

Domingo groans when he sees that Jimmy is in his group. "I don't want to work with him," Domingo says to Ms. Cox. "Get him out of my group!"

Ms. Cox walks over to Domingo and asks him, "What is wrong? You know we respect everyone in the class and we try to get along."

"He stole my lunch money," Domingo blurts out. "I don't want to be near that thief!"

"You can't prove that," Jimmy mumbles as he turns red.

I don't have to prove it," retorts Domingo. "I have three witnesses who saw you take it from my book bag."

(Continued)

(Continued)

> Jimmy stands up menacingly and begins walking toward Domingo.
> "Sit down," yells Ms. Cox as she runs toward the phone in the room.
> Domingo turns to face Jimmy as the rest of the class begins to move their desks away from the impending fight.
> Jimmy pulls a Swiss army knife from his pocket and flashes it in front of Domingo's nose. Domingo does not back down, and Jimmy inches closer.
> One of the boys in the class holds out his foot and trips Jimmy.
> Just as Jimmy begins to scuffle with the student who tripped him, the coach in the next room, who has heard the scuffle, runs into the classroom. He grabs Jimmy, Domingo, and the student who stuck his foot out and hauls them all down to the dean's office.

Solving the Problem

Students who display aggressive behavior are often trying to gain control over their lives. When students constantly utilize anger in an attempt to dominate other students or the group, they are incapable of finding a workable solution to their problems. Their inability to communicate causes them to try to overpower, intimidate, or hurt others. If students are taught to disagree with the idea and not the person, to negotiate, to discuss, and to compromise, aggressive behavior can be prevented. Anger can either be talked out or acted out. When students act out anger, aggression is the result.

> A disinterested student rarely has a satisfying picture of school in his head; perhaps he has the picture of spending his days on the street "hanging out." But if his parents are able to force him to go to school, he may choose the angry behavior of disrupting to the extent that he is suspended. Now, out on suspension, he is satisfied. In school he was frustrated and he disrupted to get closer to the picture that he wants. On the street he is in control; in school he has almost no effective control at all. (Glasser, 1986, p. 53)

Jones and Jones (2001) recommend that teachers do not become emotional or display visible anger when dealing with a student who is demonstrating aggressive behavior. When a teacher begins turning red, speaking louder and faster, and getting upset, the student is so busy thinking about the teacher that he cannot think about his own mistake or make a new plan of behavior.

The Teacher Behavior Continuum

Wolfgang, Bennett, and Irvin (1999) contrast what they call the clear-cut recipe approach to responding to misbehavior with their approach of the Teacher Behavior Continuum (TBC). Rather than writing a student's name on the board and making checkmarks each time the student commits the same offense, they believe a teacher should use an orderly arrangement of teacher techniques that correlate to the degree of power that is needed under the circumstances.

Wolfgang et al. (1999) believe that the strategy employed by the teacher should vary according to each student and the teacher's knowledge as to which techniques are most effective. In some cases, just looking at or signaling the student could be all that is needed to make the student aware of her actions. At other times, depending on the seriousness of the infraction and the purpose of the act (power play, attention getting, revenge), a teacher may need to issue a command and articulate the explicit consequence for not following the command. Figure 4.11 outlines several strategies that teachers can use to make students aware of their actions.

Even though school violence is a critical issue, serious discipline problems such as assaults, destruction of property, and a clear defiance of the teacher's authority are rare events in most schools, occurring only about 5 percent of the time. Jones (as cited in Wolfgang et al., 1999) documents that

> 80 percent of all discipline problems involve off-task behavior of students talking to others when they should be working. The second most common form is goofing off or out-of-seat behaviors (15 percent), followed by such misbehaviors as note passing, playing with items smuggled into class, and tying shoelaces. (p. 37)

Figure 4.11 Teacher Behavior Continuum (TBC)

Step 1: Looking

In the first (minimum power) behavior on the TBC, the teacher uses a modality of looking, touch, or sound to signal the student to become aware of his or her own actions.

Step 2: Naming

In the second behavior on the TBC, the teacher uses words to describe the feelings, problem, or situation the student is facing regarding some episode (e.g., difficulty with another person or objects and materials).

Step 3: Questioning

In the third teacher behavior on the TBC, the student is called on to reflect on the situation and to think of new ideas to solve the situation; alternatively, questioning could be the teacher's offer to provide assistance.

Step 4: Commanding

In the fourth behavior on the TBC, the teacher makes a powerful direct statement, telling the student what to do. Promise a Consequence is a subbehavior under the larger category of Commanding. Once the teacher has told the student what to do and sees that the student is not complying, the teacher verbally gives a promise of consequence—a promise to follow up with a strong action (physical intervention) if the student does not quickly comply.

Step 5: Acting (Physical Intervention)

In this strongest and most intrusive behavior on the TBC, the teacher physically takes the student by the hand and restricts his or her body to stop an action that is occurring.

Reprinted with permission from Wolfgang et al. (1999). *Strategies for teaching self-discipline in the middle grades,* p. 15. Boston: Allyn & Bacon.

Jones adds that a serious discipline problem usually means taking five minutes or less to send the student to the office, whereas the minor disruption or the "nickel-and-dime" actions can eat up one-third or more of total class time. It is evident, therefore, that teachers need to develop strategies to keep students on task to raise academic achievement.

Of course, all the steps listed in the Teacher Behavior Continuum help diffuse the immediate aggressive situation, but the next steps involve meeting with the student and perhaps the counselor and/or the parents. The behavior needs to be analyzed as to what provoked it, and some form of behavioral interventions, checkpoints, or conferences need to be set up to monitor the student's ability to prevent future disturbances. In many cases, the aggressive outburst was merely a symptom of a more complex issue that needs to be articulated and addressed before the aggressive behavior stops.

Bullying

Roberts (2006) believes that the terms *bullying, teasing, taunting, victimization, hazing,* and *harassment* are similar incidents or situations that vary only in intensity along a continuum of behaviors. He says that taunting is a severe form of teasing in which the aggressor does not stop when asked. He believes that

> bullying, on the other hand, is often a combination of verbal and physical aggressions and aggravations directed from an **agent** (the bully) toward a **target** (the victim). Bullying often involves direct physical contact between the bully and the victim and should be considered a higher level of concern for interveners. (p. 14)

Both teasing and bullying can inflict long-term damage on the mental health of their victims, especially if they do not receive any assistance to offset the harassment.

Roberts (2006) describes six types of students who are at risk for victimization. In general, victims (1) are *social isolates* and *outcasts,* (2) have a *transient school history,* (3) exhibit *poor social skills,* (4) *desire to fit in* "at any cost," (5) are defenseless, and (6) are viewed by their peers as different (p. 31). Unfortunately, the advent of the Internet and MySpace.com have led to cyberbullying and "cybertaunting," where victims have been subjected to embarrassing pictures and words posted on websites or sent through e-mail, instant messaging, and cell phones.

Shore (2005) discusses how being taunted or attacked physically can be one of the most painful experiences of childhood and can leave lasting psychological scars. He says that

> victims of bullying may experience anxiety, low self-esteem, depression and in some cases even suicidal thoughts. They may come to view school, where most incidents of bullying take place, as an unsafe, anxiety-provoking environment and may be afraid of attending. Some may even refuse to go to school rather than face the ordeal of bullying." (p. 5)

In addition, bullying affects the students who witness the incidents, and it often causes a climate of fear and anxiety in the school. Obviously, students won't be able to concentrate on standards and student achievement when their basic need for safety is not being met. The teacher who has set a cooperative classroom climate, taught and revisited the social skills, uses his with-it-ness scrutiny of any impending problems can monitor potential "bullying" activity and, if not prevent it, at least address it immediately, before it destroys individual students and the atmosphere of the classroom.

Violent behavior problems cannot be handled by assigning a detention or writing students' names on the board. Teachers need to work with students to develop a long-term action plan. When a student uses a weapon or attempts to use a weapon, she is usually suspended or expelled, depending upon the school's rules. Other aggressive behaviors, however, include students' threatening others, using their fists, or using their books or a desk in a violent fashion. The teacher needs to react quickly to protect the other students, then work toward solving the long-term problem of the student's aggressive behavior when or if the student returns to class. Figure 4.12 shows a sample Action Plan for the scenario described, and Figure 4.13 offers a template that teachers can use to help their students.

Other Strategies Teachers Can Use With Students With Aggressive Behaviors

- After the student returns from suspension or expulsion, talk privately with him to find out why he behaves so aggressively with other students. Try to get to the cause of the problem by asking what personal issues may be causing the behavior. Perhaps a counselor needs to be involved if home problems involve abuse or parental problems.
- Call the student's parents and find out if she has displayed any aggressive tendencies at home or in other school situations, discuss possible solutions, and schedule follow-up conferences.
- Talk with the school counselor to see if there are any previous behavior problems on the student's record. See if a special education class or special counseling is warranted.
- Give the student the option of going to the time-out or satellite area to work on his own when the pressure builds. He should be responsible for all work, but he should do it individually, without assistance from the group.
- Set up a verbal or nonverbal signal that gives the student a warning that she is losing control. For example, one hand across another showing she has "crossed the line."
- Review the behaviors of the other students in the class to see if he is particularly aggravated by one of them and is, therefore, acting out because of a personality conflict.
- Build a personal relationship with the student by talking with her and discovering her special interests.
- Evaluate his academic status to see if he feels inadequate and is resorting to aggressive behavior to compensate for his inability to keep up with the rest of the group.
- Change the cooperative group frequently so she doesn't build up a long-standing feud.

Figure 4.12 Action Plan

Analyze the problem and create an Action Plan for the incident.

**Focus
Strategy**

Students: Jimmy, Domingo, Paul

Problem: Jimmy pulled an Army knife on another student.

Quick-Recovery Actions

1. I can separate the students (unless it poses a danger for me or other students).

2. I can call for help (or send a student for help).

3. I can talk calmly to Jimmy to see if he'll drop the knife.

4. I can tell the rest of the students to leave the classroom (remove the audience).

Next-Step Actions

1. Conference with both students to find out what caused the problem.

2. It may be better to talk to the students separately to get both sides of the story.

3. Talk to the boy who tripped Jimmy.

4. Find out about the lunch money incident.

5. Get separate statements from all students involved.

Long-Term Solutions

1. Ask a peer mediator or counselor to mediate the conflict about the lunch money.

2. Reteach social skills dealing with conflict resolution to the whole class.

3. Carefully select groups for a while to avoid personality conflicts.

4. Refer Jimmy to counseling when he returns from suspension or expulsion.

Teacher: *Ms. Cox*   Date: *Sept. 25*

Figure 4.13 Action Plan Template

Students:	
Problem:	

Quick-Recovery Actions

Next-Step Actions

Long-Term Solutions

- Have students keep a checklist to keep track of their own antisocial behaviors. Then conference with them at the end of the period, day, or week about how they did and what strategies could help them.
- Videotape or audiotape a class and play it back to the student to let him see how other people perceive his behavior.
- Have the student keep a journal or log where she writes about how she feels when she is upset or angry.
- Assign him a task in which he will succeed to increase his self-esteem.
- While reviewing social skills, role-play a simulated incident involving an aggressive situation and have a discussion about how students should handle the problem.

Add some of your own solutions for helping students with aggressive behaviors:

_____

_____

_____

_____

_____

STUDENTS WHO FEEL INADEQUATE

Scenario

> Mr. Williams's world history class is studying Greek mythology. The students all have their books open as he calls on various students to read the myths.
> "Jamie, will you please read the myth about Aphrodite and Cupid for the class?" Mr. Williams asks.
> Jamie turns three shades of red and starts to read slowly and haltingly.
> "Aph-ro-dite was very vain. She spent a lot of time primp-ing and gazing in a mirror. On Mount Olymp-us [pause] she lived in a gold palace with her . . .
> "I can't pronounce the next word," Jamie mumbles under her breath. "Protégé," offers Mr. Williams.
> "Can somebody else read," begs Jamie. "I don't feel well."
> "Sure," Mr. Williams answers. "Lucas, will you please take over where Jamie left off?" Jamie puts her head down on the desk for the rest of the class.

Solving the Problem

Students often play the "I can't" game because they feel they cannot accomplish a task perfectly. Some "inadequate" students need to realize that it's okay to be imperfect. They can still cooperate with others, perform tasks reasonably well, and produce products that are acceptable.

Dinkmeyer and Losoncy (1980) say that inadequate students often say "I can't" when what they really mean is "I won't." "I can't" is a form of passive resistance, whereas "I won't" is a form of active resistance that usually provokes a power struggle or challenge to teachers. According to Dinkmeyer and Losoncy, "the 'I can't' phrase suggests helplessness and can serve the following purposes:

1. One believes others should serve him or her and puts others in service by proclaiming inadequacy.

2. One believes that he or she is an inadequate person and protects himself or herself from possible failure by 'copping out'—avoiding facing life's challenges.

3. One believes that he or she is unable, helpless, and should be excused from being expected to function. (pp. 55–56)

Often students who feel inadequate lack confidence in their ability and perceive life as unfair because while they may try very hard, but their efforts still lead to failure. These students become discouraged and develop negative self-concepts. In some cases, these students totally withdraw and give up completely (Dinkmeyer & Losoncy, 1980). Teachers often let these quiet and withdrawn students slip through the cracks because they are too busy managing the noisier students who are seeking attention or power. Unfortunately, the discouraged and inadequate block of students is much larger than most people realize, and these quiet students often become dropout statistics. In more cases than not, the roots of their difficulties can be traced to learning problems. Students who cannot read would rather refuse to read or appear uninterested rather than read in the class and embarrass themselves in front of their peers. Bellanca and Fogarty (2003) offer tactics to help inadequate students feel confident and in control (see Figure 4.14).

Figure 4.14 Tactics Teachers Can Use With Students Who Feel Inadequate

- Assign tasks that the student can successfully complete.
- Talk with the student to analyze why he or she feels inadequate.
- Pair the inadequate student with an empathetic student who can help.
- Lower the student's anxiety about mistakes.
- De-emphasize grades and emphasize a love of learning.
- Break larger tasks into small chunks (checklists).
- Remind students of past successes.
- Use team-building activities to build trust among group members.
- Arrange for homework buddies so the student gets additional help and support.
- Give positive feedback.

Some students who feel inadequate come to teachers with pessimistic expectations that have been ingrained in them since early childhood. Teachers will not always be able to lift the heavy weight from their shoulders after only one or two conferences. Persistence is the key to helping the student who feels inadequate feel successful, become a valuable member of the group, do well on whole-group activities, and succeed on individual tasks. These students try to avoid anything that could cause them to fail; therefore, the teacher's role is to structure activities that will make the student succeed, gain confidence, and develop a positive self-concept. Giving the students checklists and rubrics to guide their efforts often provides them with a road map to success and reduces their anxiety about not "knowing what the teacher wants."

One strategy teachers can use is to read between the lines to determine the real cause of a problem. A student could be acting out or withdrawing to cover a real problem that is causing him to feel insecure or inadequate. Sometimes a one-on-one private teacher-student conference can help teachers discover how best to help the student.

The key to effective problem solving in a conference is reflective listening. Teachers who use closed questions that call for a yes or no answer and who begin with the word *why* tend to cut off true communication.

Closed Questions

Closed questions sound accusatory, somewhat sarcastic, and negative. They antagonize students and put them on the defensive. The smart responses students sometimes give the teacher are in retaliation for the teacher's embarrassing them in front of their peers. Even if students say nothing or reply courteously, they have suffered humiliation, and their self-esteem has been lowered. It is doubtful that closed questions will motivate students to shape up. Some sample closed questions are given in Figure 4.15.

Open Questions

Open questions invite further conversation and many possible responses. They also help establish a rapport between teacher and student because they convey to the student a sense of caring and fairness (see Figure 4.16).

Figure 4.15 Sample Closed Questions

Question:	"Are you just going to sit there, or are you going to get busy?"
Answer:	"Yes, I'm going to sit here—what are you going to do about it?"
Question:	"Do you really think you're funny?"
Answer:	"Yes, I do think I'm funny!"
Question:	"Why don't you stop fooling around and get on task?"
Answer:	"Because I'm not quite finished fooling around yet."

Figure 4.16 Sample Open Questions

Question:	"So, you're saying that you're upset because you don't think you read well?"
Answer:	"I am not sure."
Question:	"Hmm. Would you like to explore some ways we can make you feel more confident when you read in front of the class?"
Answer:	"Yes, I would!"

As the teacher listens to the student talk about the problem, she may want to listen for and draw out the following "subtexts."

- Could it be that the student would like other students to notice her more?
- Could it be that other students tease her about reading out loud?
- Could it be that she has a language problem that embarrasses her?

Dreikurs recommends that during such a discussion, teachers look carefully at the student for what he calls a "recognition reflex," or an involuntary sign that the guess is correct. The reflex could be a shift in posture, a change in eye contact, or a nonverbal cue that indicates the underlying reason for the problem. Often, the student is not aware of what the real problem is, and it's the teacher's job to bring it to the surface (cited in Dinkmeyer et al., 1980, p. 114).

As shown in the focus strategy in Figure 4.17, teachers may want to include parents in the plan for solving the problem and bolstering the student's self-esteem. Figure 4.18 contains a Teacher-Student Conference template that teachers can use with their students.

Even though teachers are extremely busy and teach many students each day, the one-on-one conference accomplishes a great deal. First, the teacher devotes individual attention to the student. Second, the teacher focuses on the problem without the distractions of the rest of the class. Third, the teacher gets to know the student on a more personal basis. The interpersonal touch goes a long way in helping students gain confidence and overcome inadequacy.

Other Strategies Teachers Can Use With Students Who Feel Inadequate

- A student may increase his self-esteem by succeeding at an extracurricular activity.
- Work out a secret system with the inadequate student. Promise the student that you will only call on her if you are standing right next to her. That way the student does not have to worry about being called on at other times and can concentrate on the lesson.
- Give the inadequate student a great deal of wait time when you ask questions. Also, try to ask questions you know he can answer to build his confidence.

Figure 4.17 Teacher-Student Conference

After the teacher asks the student a series of open questions, both the teacher and the student fill out this form.

Focus Strategy

Student: _____*Jamie*_____   Teacher: _____*Mr. Williams*_____   Date: _____*Sept. 9*_____

Teacher's concern: _*I am concerned because you don't participate in class discussions and*_
*you always seem to get sick or have some other excuse whenever I call on you in class to read*
*or answer a question.*

Student's concern: _*I am really shy, and I don't like to talk in class because I'm afraid I might*_
*say something stupid and the other kids will laugh at me. I also hate to read out loud. I get really*
*nervous, and I don't understand one thing I read because I'm thinking about pronouncing*
*things wrong or not knowing the words.*

Possible options:

1. _*Mr. Williams will not call on Jamie unless she has her hand raised.*_
2. _*Mr. Williams will not call on students to read in front of the whole class. He'll either put students*_
   *in groups of 2 or 3 to read together or allow them to read silently.*
3. _*Jamie will go to the reading teacher to get tested to see if she needs extra help.*_

Parent involvement: *I will have Jamie read out loud to me every night to help her feel more comfortable with pronouncing words and reading out loud. I will also buy some audio tapes of stories for her to listen to as she reads.*

Parent's signature: _____*Mrs. Hansen*_____

Date of next conference: _____*Sept. 22*_____

Figure 4.18 Teacher-Student Conference Template

Student: _____   Teacher: _____   Date: _____

Teacher's concern: _____
_____
_____
_____
_____

Student's concern: _____
_____
_____
_____
_____

Possible options:

1. _____
   _____

2. _____
   _____

3. _____
   _____

Parent involvement:

Parent's signature: _____

Date of next conference: _____

- Give specific encouragement for the student's accomplishment. In other words, don't just say "Great speech." Tell the student the speech was great because she used good eye contact, effective gestures, and appropriate humor.
- Make sure to allow enough time for each activity. Inadequate students often feel rushed, and they become frustrated when the teacher and the class are moving faster than they are.
- Leave some time between activities so students can make the transition. Inadequate students may also suffer from learning disabilities, and they have a difficult time changing their mind-set quickly from one task to another.
- Make sure all homework assignments are realistic. Do not give excessive amounts of homework because inadequate students get very frustrated when they cannot complete all the work. It takes them longer to complete assignments than other students.
- Do not give new material for homework because students might not understand the new concepts. The homework should be a review of concepts already studied.
- Provide checklists for rubrics for all major assignments so that students know the expectations for quality work.

Add some of your own solutions for helping students who feel inadequate:

_____

_____

_____

_____

_____

5

Dealing
With Difficult
Students

Donna Walker Tileston

While the ideas provided in the previous chapters work most of the time, there are always those times when we need to move to Plan B. Not all off-task problems in the classroom are minor. While there are many reasons for student behavior, most writers place the types of negative behavior into basic categories for discussion. Let's look at some of the categories of negative behavior and the characteristics that usually accompany those behaviors.

STUDENTS WHO WANT ATTENTION

Students who are not getting the attention that they want (or need) through normal means may resort to off-task, attention-getting behavior to accomplish their goal. Some of the ways in which they exhibit this behavior include:

- Being late for class
- Speaking out without permission

- Making noises
- Talking out of turn
- Getting up from their desks or chairs to walk around or to go to the pencil sharpener, trashcan, and so forth, for the third or fourth time
- Intentionally breaking the rules

When needs are not met, the behavior may escalate to:

- Shouts and verbal attacks
- Defiance of authority

You will know this behavior by the effect that it has on you, the teacher: "When attention is the reason for the misbehavior, you will generally feel annoyed" (Master Teacher, 2002).

While there is no single solution to the attention-getting behavior of some of our students, examining some of the reasons for this behavior may help in finding solutions. These students are often kinesthetic learners or highly visual learners who have difficulty in a classroom where the dominant teaching method is auditory. By bringing in visuals, models of the learning, and providing movement, the classroom teacher may be able to solve this dilemma. Boredom often causes off-task, attention-getting behavior. Ask yourself, is this student being challenged? Have students been required to sit and listen for long periods of time? Brain researchers agree that our brain is not wired to attend to lecture-type formats for long periods of time. For students 15 years old through adult, 20 minutes seems to be the maximum time that we will pay attention in one segment. For students under 15, their age is a good measurement. For example, an eight-year-old will listen for about eight minutes before fading out. Have you been in a meeting in which someone talked to you for an hour or more? Did you notice yourself drifting in and out of the meeting even if the information was something of interest to you?

Help attention seekers to find fulfillment of their needs by providing feedback and lots of praise when they are working well. These students are like those people who pour quarters into video games—they do better when they have immediate feedback and instant gratification. These students also must be explicitly taught how to use the metacognitive system more appropriately, especially in regard to following through on tasks.

When working with students who want attention, it is important to remember the following points to turn the behavior around:

- Be direct and to the point. Tell them exactly what they did wrong, what the consequence is, and why.
- Lighten up. Smile or use humor when dealing with these students.
- Use negotiation when appropriate. For example, tell them that you will not lecture for more than ten minutes at a time and that you will provide opportunities for movement and for talking with other students through small groups or pairing of students at the end of each ten-minute segment. (This is a much more brain-friendly way to teach, anyway.)
- Provide opportunities for students to move during the class time. If working in groups is not appropriate to the learning, provide times when students can stand and stretch.

Students Who Seek Power

Characteristics of students who seek power may include some or all of the following:

- Demonstrates anxiety
- May be tired often or have headaches
- May try to use guilt to get control
- Nags and complains often
- Tries to control the teacher or others in the classroom
- Has an authoritarian attitude

"When power is the reason for the misbehavior, you will generally feel threatened" (Master Teacher, 2002).

The play for power is usually made out of fear—fear of failure, fear of not being accepted, fear of consequences, and more. The teacher is usually the one with the most power in the classroom. After all, in the eyes of the students, this is the person who can give detentions, call parents, take away points, and give extra work. Interestingly, these are sometimes students who are very structured and who feel that the classroom does not provide enough structure or that discipline is not being maintained. These students will literally take over if intervention is not made promptly. Some ways that the classroom teacher can deal with this behavior is first to have very specific structures in place for work and behavior and to be consistent in their enforcement. Second, the teacher who provides choices for students and who involves students in classroom decisions is less likely to have this type of problem in the classroom. Getting into a power play with a student is a lose/lose situation. Even if you win, you will probably come across as a bully. A more powerful way to deal with these students is to listen to their concerns, acknowledge their feelings, and deal with the issue in private. If they complain loudly about you, let it go in one ear and out the other. Do not give in to the urge to get into a power struggle in front of the class. Help this student to see other choices in the situation. Payne (2001) says in working with inner-city students to have them write down other choices and which choice they will take next time. Glasser (1986) says students sometimes feel the need for power in the classroom because they feel that no one is listening to them. Students who are not doing well academically will especially feel that they are unimportant to the system. Burke (1992) uses a graphic model to help analyze conflicts with students who seek power. For older students, this tool could be used as the basis of a discussion to help them see their behavior and to help analyze those factors that will help to diffuse the situation (see Figure 5.1).

When working with students who seek power, the following guide may help to diffuse the behavior:

- Use direct honesty. Tell them exactly what the behavior looks like and sounds like. If you beat around the bush, they will know.
- Be factual. This is what you are doing and here are the indicators. These students do not want "I think and I feel"; they operate on facts.
- Refer back to the rules. These students usually like perimeters and rules and they like for them to be carried out. More than any other group, this group needs to see the rules and needs any disciplinary action to follow the rules.
- State the problem, the rules, and the consequences—in writing.

Figure 5.1   Phases of a Power Struggle

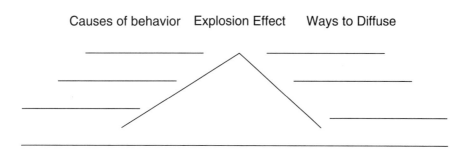

Causes of behavior   Explosion Effect   Ways to Diffuse

STUDENTS WHO WANT REVENGE

Some characteristics of students who seek revenge include:

- Critical of the classroom, other students, or the teacher
- Argumentative
- Questions why often
- Aloof or withdrawn, may even daydream
- Snobbish
- May do things his or her own way instead of the way that was assigned
- Critical of the rules, especially if they are inconsistent or if they are not enforced

When their behavior is out of control, it will manifest itself in acts of meanness or spitefulness such as beating up another student or defacing property. You will know the behavior by the way that it makes you feel. Most teachers will feel fearful or angry.

> Sometimes power seekers who never satisfy their need for power become revenge seekers to "get back" at the person or persons who thwarted their quest for power. Usually the revengeful student is trying to retaliate for something hurtful said by a parent, teacher, or peer or for some injustice or unfair deed. (Burke, 1992, p. 194)

The injustice may not have been done to the person seeking revenge—it may have been something that involved another student or the whole classroom. These students should be listened to and they should be taken seriously. Punitive actions toward this behavior will just accelerate the behavior in the student. The problem needs to be dealt with privately and in an adult voice—no put-downs, no sarcasm. These behaviors are sometimes manifested in some of our best students, especially if they feel that a wrong has been committed. These students can make the classroom a miserable place to be when they use their abilities to torpedo the climate in the classroom.

When working with students who seek revenge, the following suggestions may help to turn the behavior around:

- Use logic with these students. For example, "If I allow everyone in the room to 'do their own thing' instead of following the rules, we will have chaos."
- Be objective and nonconfrontational. Show respect for the student, not for the behavior.
- Acknowledge their contributions to the classroom.
- Provide opportunities for independent activities from time to time to help satisfy their need to do things their own way.

STUDENTS WHO FEEL INADEQUATE

Some of the characteristics of these students include:

- May ignore the teacher
- Does not participate
- May threaten to quit
- Tends to over-react to events
- May come to class unprepared or may not work to ability level
- Moody, blames others for failure

This behavior exhibited by your students may cause you to feel frustration.

These students are easy to spot in the classroom. Their emotions are usually on the outside. They may be more sensitive than other students and at times can be very caring of others. These students need frequent feedback about how they are doing, and they need positive encouragement. Often these are the underachievers who feel that they have no locus of control. They try hard but cannot experience success. Their frustration is manifested in tears, mentally dropping out, pouting, bursts of anger, or giving the teacher the silent treatment. The anxiety level needs to be lowered for these students by talking with them about why they feel inadequate, providing feedback and encouragement, and being sure that they have the necessary prerequisite skills before putting them into independent learning situations. Self-efficacy is the key to helping these students—provide incremental opportunities for these students to be successful, beginning with simple tasks with minimum challenge and working to high challenge but keeping low to moderate stress.

Some ideas for working with students who are motivated by feelings of inadequacy include:

- Talk to the student privately and in a calm tone.
- Listen to the student's side of the story.

- Keep communications open. These students usually like to talk and will shut down communication with you when they feel threatened.
- Help them to see the relevance of the learning, especially how it will help them personally and how it will help others.
- These students need feedback often, so to the extent possible, provide feedback throughout the class period.

For those problems that are motivated by anger, fear, revenge, or the need for power, we need a back-up plan. This plan should be built around planning for behavior problems and knowing in advance how you will handle them. When you have a plan, it is more likely that you will not explode or say something that will be difficult to follow up. Let me begin by telling you some things NOT to do.

- Do not lose your temper, even when students make comments about you or the classroom. Do not take it personally. Practice letting comments go in one ear and out the other. Before responding, count one hundred one, one hundred two, one hundred three. Take a breath and relax. Fred Jones (2002) says that we tend to move our hands above our waist when we are angry and we keep our hands at our side when we are relaxed. Practice being relaxed even when the situation is tense. Practice with your colleagues or family—anyone who is willing to help you learn to pace yourself and remain cool. If you take the comments personally, the situation is much more likely to escalate.
- Do not make idle threats. Never threaten action you cannot carry out. Even if you can carry out the threat, do not make it to the whole class—make it privately to the person(s) involved.
- Do not put names on the board. That just alienates the students.
- Do not humiliate the student.

- Do not ignore poor behavior. The class knows the behavior is inappropriate, and if you ignore it, the class will assume that behavior is not a priority with you.
- Never treat one student differently from another. Behavior management should be consistent and fair.

What if the discipline problems are persistent and/or not related to motivation? How should we deal with disruptive behavior?

Here are some guidelines for what to do to change disruptive behavior (based, in part, on the research of Fred Jones, available at www.fredjones.com).

1. Stay calm. Do not let your body language or your face betray the tension that you feel. Take time to calm down (even though it may seem like a long time, try giving yourself three seconds by counting one hundred one, one hundred two, one hundred three). Put your arms at your sides loosely and keep your jaw loose by running your tongue over the roof of your mouth.

2. Look toward the person or persons being disruptive. If that does not get them back to work, walk toward them.

3. When you have reached the student, put your palms down on the desk and speak quietly to the student. When the student gets back to work, remove your palms from the desk and slowly turn and leave. You should be cruising the room to help students and to see their work so that the students do not view this activity as an interruption. As a matter of fact, if done correctly, the students will not even be aware that you have disciplined a student.

4. Be sure that students who have been disruptive turn completely around to their work and have their feet under their desks. Students who turn only partially are probably planning to talk to their friends as soon as you walk away.

5. If a student makes a negative comment as you start to leave, calmly turn around and repeat the procedure you just did with that student. Do not answer the comment—why escalate the situation and allow them the victory of getting you angry? You must do something when the comment is made to get the student back on task, because not only have you heard the comment but so have students around you. They will be watching to see if you give in to the student.

6. Keep anecdotal notes in your grade book or in a separate notebook to help you keep up with encounters in case you must bring in parents or administration.

7. If you feel the behavior needs further discussion, ask the student to stay after class so that you may talk.

8. Keep your own file of students' names, addresses, phone numbers, and how to reach parents.

9. Ask for a copy of the discipline procedure policies for your school and read it from cover to cover. There should be steps for what to do when the behavior has moved beyond isolated incidents.

10. Your best plan is to be prepared. Know how you will react in given situations and follow through.

11. If your school does not have a plan for emergencies such as when a student's behavior becomes bizarre or beyond what you are able to handle (this includes fist fights in the classroom), make a plan with a teacher nearby so that you have a code for help. For example, you might cut out an apple and laminate it. When the situation becomes tense, you might ask a student pleasantly to take the apple to Mr. Wilcox next door. We have also used code words such as calling into the office and saying it is Washington's birthday or Betty Boop so that they know there is a problem. If you do not have a phone in your room, ask a student to go to the room next door to tell the teacher a secret word

that you have worked out in advance. The point is to be prepared. It is much easier to stay calm in an emergency if you have a plan and if you have thought out the situations.

A Few Words About Anger

Panksepp (1998) identifies anger as "that powerful force we experience as an internal pressure to reach out and strike someone." In this time of great anxiety and stress, we are seeing the lack of impulsivity control more and more from road rage to fist fights. The classroom is no exception. Not only do we see anger acted upon daily, but anger often moves to rage when needs are not met or when the student feels trapped. Given (2002) says, "Rage occurs as a result of being stuck in a fear-flight response when attempts to flee a fearful situation are thwarted." Scientists have found that people with serious aggression usually have low levels of seratonin and high levels of norepinephrine. These chemicals seem to increase the general arousal effects of anger and aggression (Linnoila et al., 1994). Explicitly helping students to examine their concept of themselves may help in lowering this negative behavior. Given (2002) says, "If educators expect students to persevere with learning tasks, then they must attend to how students view themselves within the classroom context." To do this takes patience and consistency. It is a commitment to students and to the community. On every national agenda are the issues of education and the issue of violence in the neighborhoods. As teachers, we have an opportunity to help solve those problems as no other individuals have. Using what we know about the self-system of the brain, we can make changes in our communities that will have long-lasting effects. By teaching students to examine themselves, their motivations, and the picture that they have of themselves, we make the first steps toward change. Given says,

If students frequently act out and are abrasive or belligerent, their own actions become internalized as defining characteristics of self as "difficult." By contrast, if students see themselves as friendly, helpful, and kind, those characteristics become internalized as a definition of self as "pleasant and caring." Students then continue to behave in ways consistent with their self-perception.

WORKING WITH STUDENTS FROM POVERTY

Most of the students who come to us from poverty are not discipline problems. However, there are characteristics that are often attributed to these students that may offer challenges to the student and the teacher. For example, Payne (2001) says that students from generational poverty (poverty for two or more generations) may laugh when disciplined because in their world this is a way to save face. Some other behaviors they may exhibit include:

- *Arguing with the teacher*—Those in poverty often distrust anyone in authority.
- *Inappropriate or vulgar comments*—Inner-city students and students from poverty use a form of language called casual register that includes words from the street.
- *Inability to follow directions*—Procedural memory is often not used in poverty. Students who have grown up in poverty tend to live for now; planning is not part of their day-to-day activities.
- *Fighting*—Fighting is often how children in poverty survive. They do not know negotiating skills because they have not been taught.
- *Hands on others*—Nonverbal data are a part of poverty. The body is important because it is one of the few things they own.

WHAT'S A TEACHER TO DO?

Most schools are run on the ethics, speech, and values of the middle class. In order to work with students from poverty, we must first understand that they may not know the rules of the middle class or why it is important for them to follow those rules. Students need to know that there is one way to be successful on the streets and another way to be successful in school and on the job. Telling students that they must never laugh in the face of fear could get them killed on the streets. We want them to survive both at school and in their neighborhoods. Help them to understand the difference and why they need to know it. Here are some other ideas that may help as you work with these students:

1. Understand the reason for the behavior.

2. Help students to see other options for their behavior while in school.

3. Provide lots of kinesthetic activities. These students will not do well in an environment where they must sit for long periods of time and listen to lecture. (Actually, few of us do well in that setting.)

4. Teach them positive self-talk. These students often come to us believing that they cannot be successful. Demonstrate for them how you use self-talk as you walk through problems. Since they do not have experience with procedures that require step-by-step directions, help them to use self-talk to walk through procedures.

5. Don't argue with the students. Instead, ask them to tell you what they did, why they did it, and another way they could do it next time. You may need to help them with options.

6. Speak to them in the adult voice. Payne (2001) defines this as a voice that is "nonjudgmental, free of negative nonverbal, factual, often in question format, and attitude of win-win." Some questions this voice might use include:
   - In what ways could this be resolved?
   - What are the choices in this situation?

- These are the consequences of that choice.
- We agree to disagree (Payne, 2001, p. 110).

In Conclusion

The four major causes of misbehavior in the classroom include the need for attention, power, revenge, and self-confidence. There are specific activities that can be identified in students that relate to each of the needs. When the needs are not met, the behavior may escalate and become difficult to control. Of the three factors involved in any discipline problem—the teacher, the student who is misbehaving, and the rest of the class—the one we can control is ourselves. It is important that we do not take the behavior personally, that we remain calm, that we take care of the behavior immediately and consistently, and that we deal with it appropriately. The Master Teacher lists seven primary physical needs that affect behavior and eight secondary needs that are physiological. The primary needs include such things as:

1. *Hunger*—Not just immediate hunger but improper nutrition, too much carbohydrate, and inadequate calories for the body to operate at an optimum level.

2. *Thirst*—Our brains need hydration, not just at intervals, but also throughout the day. Inadequate fluid intake has an immediate reaction on the brain and learning. The use of certain drugs can also cause excess thirst in students.

3. *Relationships*—With the teacher, other students, or anyone outside of the classroom may be the underlying cause of misbehavior.

4. *Space and other physical factors*—The classroom itself may be the problem. Inadequate lighting, heat, air, or resources affect behavior.

5. *Rest and breaks from routine*—Even the most interesting

of subjects can become boring when the body has not had adequate rest or breaks in the learning. Provide opportunities for students to talk to one another, to take breaks, and opportunities for think time.

6. *Fear of pain*—Pain can be physical or emotional, and both can inhibit learning. The teacher should be aware of conditions within the classroom that facilitate emotional pain and work to eliminate them.

7. *Need for a restroom break*—Some students are too shy to ask to be excused. Make sure that you have a plan in place for going to the restroom and that the fear that someone might take advantage of the plan does not overshadow providing opportunities for students to leave the room.

When the underlying problem does not fall into any of the seven primary reasons listed above, look to the four motivators of power, attention, revenge, or lack of self-esteem for the underlying cause. Before dealing with the behavior, seek to identify what it is and the possible causes so that you can more effectively deal with it on a permanent basis. Changing behavior is not just a quick fix; it should be an opportunity to help students see their behavior for what it is and to find positive ways to satisfy the need.

Table 5.1 can act as a guide as you identify behaviors in your classroom.

Table 5.1   Identify the Problem Behavior

Revenge	Power	Self-Concept	Attention
Defaces property	Refuses to follow rules	Emotional	Speaks out without permission
Fights or bullies	Criticizes	Will not participate	Gets up without permission
Argues	Bosses other students	Blames others for failure	Class clown
Does things own way	Tries to take over class	Threatens to drop out	Makes noises to entertain

CHAPTER SIX

Understanding The RCM Plan™

J. Allen Queen and Bob Algozzine

Teach the three Rs: Respect for yourself, Responsibility for your actions, and Remembering the rights of others.

—Robert Algozzine,
from *Teacher's Little Book of Wisdom*

A HIGH SCHOOL CLASSROOM SCENE

To Rosemary Lopez, the new social studies teacher at Washington High, the early morning hall was alive with the usual noises: lockers slamming, friends yelling one more reminder as they charged in opposite directions, and too many feet dragging on the tiled floor. Next to Ms. Lopez's classroom, Lisa and Jon were right behind the door, whispering very seriously and holding each other as they did yesterday and the days before that. Clearly, school was not their primary concern, and Ms. Lopez's greeting only heightened their whispering. The indifference to education here was palpable.

Placing her coffee on her desk, Ms. Lopez was pleased to see that almost everybody was at their assigned desks—except, of course, Lisa and Jon, still holding, and Yoko and Robert, who were arguing in the back of the room. With the bell, Ms. Lopez expected full attention from the class,

(Continued)

(Continued)

and asked Thomas, sitting next to the door, to request Lisa and Jon's presence. Thomas, out of his seat before she even asked, attended to this regular early morning assignment. Yoko and Robert increased the volume of their exchange until Ms. Lopez could no longer restrain herself. She spoke to them as sternly as possible without showing her temper, yet was aware that her pitch was too high for effective intimidation; but somehow, she had to gain control. As the class watched nervously, she sarcastically asked Lisa and Jon if their marriage was faltering. The stratagem seemed to distract them. Yoko laughed, while Jon took offense and answered with a wisecrack about Ms. Lopez's ethnic group. His male friends hooted in approval . . . again, business as usual.

Ignoring the bait, Ms. Lopez asked the class to take out the individual assignments they had been working on for the last week. She could only hope that she had gotten on the right side of the contest by scoring a slight victory, temporary as it would be.

Damon waved his hand at Ms. Lopez and asked to present his materials first. Ms. Lopez looked around at the other hands, noting the expressions of those who did not volunteer as withdrawn and indifferent. She decided to ignore them; she could not afford to waste what little productive time she had to extract what they probably did not know anyway.

So, she quickly agreed to Damon's insistence, trying to move rapidly into the lesson without further distraction. Nevertheless, Robert asked, tauntingly, why he never got a chance to go first. Ms. Lopez saw her chance to embarrass Robert and asked Damon to allow Robert to demonstrate his knowledge. Robert said that he and Yoko had done the work together. Ms. Lopez replied that she was not interested in group work. She wanted to know what he was capable of—what he had done. Robert responded with sarcasm; this time directed at Damon. Kabir, Damon's friend, stared hard at Robert. Ms. Lopez felt her control become increasingly precarious.

Pushing hard ahead, Ms. Lopez proffered a short introduction, describing how she expected the class to carry on the discussion. The "squawk box" interrupted the effort with innocuous announcements. Ms. Lopez started over, clearly frustrated by the further delay. The class took precious minutes to refocus. Ms. Lopez then asked Damon to read his paper on the assigned issue of world population. She hoped the material would engage the class in something she considered important and immediate. She knew she was taking a chance, but the topic was in the news and certainly entwined in the study of world cultures. Within a few minutes, she realized she was right and wrong. The class was listening to Damon, but the class was also getting agitated as he confronted their preconceptions. They increasingly attacked his position and virtually everything he was saying.

Ms. Lopez recognized she needed to keep a tight lid on the discussion—quite opposite to what she had hoped. These discussions were laced with threads of racial, ethnic, and class conflict. She knew the backgrounds of her students; and, for many, she could guess their social and economic status. But as she looked at her class more closely, she realized that she did not really know them; she had not shared their experiences. She did not understand the extraordinary diversity of background, ability, and interest that confronted her. What could she do with this situation to make it work? Did she have the training? Did she have the skill? Could she succeed? What could she do to reclaim classroom management and teach effectively?

THE RCM PLAN™

The classroom scene illustrates a few moments of the complex dynamics and inherent potential for conflict in middle or secondary school classrooms in the United States today. Undoubtedly, this image is disquieting, but real. Compared to a decade ago, societal and personal conditions are more complex, harder to grasp, and more difficult to control. The nation's public schools absorb the pace and degree of these changes, and the individual classroom teacher stands at the core of the expected change process. The teacher likely depicts the perfect panacea capable of clearly manifesting the stability needed for behavioral and academic changes in our students. It is in this context that we introduce The Responsible Classroom Management Plan (The RCM Plan™).

The RCM Plan™ is a schoolwide, behavior-correcting plan that enhances a school's capacity to safely and effectively educate all students. The RCM Plan™ applies evidence-based support systems to maximize opportunities for teaching academics and prosocial behaviors. The following characteristics are embedded in the plan (Horner, Sugai, Todd, & Lewis-Palmer, 2005; Sugai, 2000; Sugai & Horner, 2002; Sugai, Sprague, Horner, & Walker, 2000):

- A team-based approach to identify, implement, and evaluate best practices, including administrators, teachers, school psychologists, other support personnel, and parents.
- Support for improvement efforts with budget, personnel, and resource allocations.
- Use of research-validated practices.
- Proactive behavioral instruction, teaching and modeling appropriate social behavior, with plenty of positive feedback.
- Opportunities for students to practice the expected behavior, aiming for fluency.
- A continuum of behavioral support to increase the intensity of the intervention as the intensity of the problem increases.
- Data-based systems and schoolwide, behavioral goals to guide decisions and keep staff informed on current guidelines along with what is and is not working.

Promoting good citizenship by developing responsible students who can live productively in a democratic and multicultural society is a key goal of responsible classroom management (RCM). This involves acting responsibly and practicing socially acceptable behavior. Responsible students also self-correct inappropriate behavior after they experience natural consequences for any inappropriate acts. William Glasser, in his book *Reality Therapy* (1990), defines responsibility as follows:

... the ability to fulfill one's needs, and to do so in a way that does not deprive others of the ability to fulfill their needs. ... A responsible person also does that which gives him a feeling of self-worth and a feeling that he is worthwhile to others. (p. xi)

Glasser believes students have certain needs that must be met by either the home or the school. When students behave inappropriately, it is because (according to Glasser) their basic needs are not being met. If the home does not satisfy those needs, then the school must try to meet them. Accordingly, the school and teachers must assist students in being successful in what they undertake—in their effort to learn, and in their pursuit of self-worth. It follows that if a student misbehaves in school, then teachers must somehow help the student meet unmet needs. If a student cannot adjust and behave more productively, then teachers must find ways to alter their own behavior, or the structure and contents of the classroom, to assist the student.

Taking a similar position to Glasser, RCM posits that teachers should not try to alter a student's world and allow the student to avoid the consequences of misbehavior. Changing the school environment is not the same as altering rules and expectations so that a student can avoid injury to self-worth. Rather, teachers should help students make value judgments about what causes a problem. When students judge their misbehavior and commit themselves to change, they will learn responsibility. Once a student commits to change, a teacher can accept no excuse from the student for not maintaining the commitment.

The RCM Plan™ ensures that a student is not permitted to escape responsibility for misbehavior. This does not mean that a teacher should punish or praise a student for a certain act, since this disconnects the student from directly accepting responsibility for the behavior. While punishment permits the student to focus on the punishment and the consequent feelings of revenge, praise motivates the student to seek similar commendation for any and all activity. Both practices thereby delay self-motivation. As an alternative, teachers must use logical consequences for the student to correct the misbehavior and develop responsibility.

BECOMING A SUCCESSFUL RCM TEACHER

To be successful, RCM teachers must analyze their own behavior to determine where they might inject unfavorable behaviors and attitudes into the classroom. Tendencies toward authoritarian or permissive control, prejudice, ignorance of the correct methodology, indecisiveness, or uncertainty about the goals of RCM will each undermine the RCM classroom and school.

According to the RCM perspective, external rewards in the form of reinforcement, or even casual praise, delay development of the responsible student. In a dynamic, creative, and uncontrived classroom, a teacher depends on the excitement from tapping a student's inherent need to know, learn, and very importantly, belong. RCM teachers derive a significant portion of stable behavior from excellence in instructional preparation and execution. Successful RCM teachers, then, carefully entwine **standards** and **guidelines** into the instructional process alongside **expected behaviors** supported by **natural and logical consequences**.

The Three Major RCM Principles

While The RCM Plan™ integrates many educational beliefs, three major principles maximize student success. These are listed and briefly addressed here, with much greater detail offered in later chapters about how these principles work in harmony to achieve all the desired behaviors discussed to this point.

The basic-program principles of The RCM Plan™ include:

1. Responsibility is taught and incorporated instructionally within a warm and inviting classroom.

The RCM approach to classroom management develops responsible students who can live productively in a democratic and multicultural society. Within the RCM classroom, responsibility is taught and then expected. Teachers, and the school organization, should implement democratic principles in their teaching and leadership roles. Human equality, dignity, self-worth, participation in decision making at all levels, and acceptance of the consequences of behavior should all be concepts integrated into the curriculum and consistently taught.

The school and classroom environment, and the concomitant instructional effort, embody the RCM approach. In a safe and inviting environment, a student feels secure and protected, and is then prepared to learn. The more positive the experience of the classroom, the greater the opportunity the teacher has to guide the students toward responsible behavior. Organization of space and time, format and presentation of instructional materials, the demeanor of the teachers, and the amount and kind of preparation are all critically important to success in an environmentally sound school and classroom. The RCM approach requires a teacher to clearly state the objectives of all planned classroom activity. This outcome-based approach to instruction necessitates the teacher's careful preparation and constant evaluation of student behavior. Precise and sensitive instructional guidance builds the foundation for responsible student behavior.

2. Standards, guidelines, and expected behaviors replace rigid school and classroom rules.

The RCM Plan™ does not use rules. Instead, the teacher uses standards, guidelines, and expected behaviors. Standards define the general direction of the desired behavior. Guidelines provide specific directions to successfully meet those standards, and expected behaviors represent grade level and developmentally appropriate actions to follow. In the RCM classroom, teachers act swiftly, consistently, and unemotionally to instill desirable behavior. As students learn to internalize responsible behavior, their self-esteem matures, and they increasingly gain internalized control over their own behavior.

3. Consequences teach students to self-correct inappropriate behaviors and assume responsibility for their actions.

Logical consequences link a student's inappropriate action to violated expected behavior, breaking the guideline and thus the standard. A logical consequence is not punishment. Instead, more realistic consequences result from not doing what is expected. For example, one guideline states, "The student is to come to school prepared to learn." In discussing this expectation, the teacher gives a directive for students to complete homework on a daily basis. Every student is expected to do the homework, with no exceptions. If a student comes in without his homework, he is not penalized with a low grade. Instead, he may be asked when he would like to complete the assignment—at break, during lunch, or after school. Those may be his only choices or there may be others. Specifically, the teacher may assign another consequence if she believes the initial one would not change the inappropriate behavior with this particular student. What happens if he doesn't have his homework in the future? One possibility is to simply repeat the consequence. Repeating a consequence can work well and proves that as teacher, she is serious. If the repeated consequence does not work, the teacher must move to something different with this student.

Individual Treatment

Within the RCM classroom, students are considered individuals who must be treated fairly and equally, but not necessarily the same. No parent disciplines two or three students in the same manner. For one student, time in her room is punishment and to another student, it is as a reward. Discipline, then, has to be personalized. Teachers achieve this with RCM and receive far less parental complaints than with other programs.

RCM fosters and acknowledges student performance and personal responsibility, and does not use bribery and predetermined rewards. Too often, teachers attempt to motivate students to learn and behave acceptably in the classroom with external rewards. This process is time-consuming, and often results in students who rely solely on extrinsic rewards to accomplish what should be intrinsically important to them. In contradistinction to this scheme, the RCM approach to classroom management uses high expectations and reasonable guidelines and standards to develop intrinsic motivation.

Students practice internal-behavior control rather than have their behavior controlled externally. Strict rules for obedience insulate students from personal responsibility—a result contrary to RCM purpose. When a student is taught to act autonomously, according to agreed-upon standards, the student acts responsibly. Responsible behavior does not require enforcement, and will likely be repeated without the application of external inducements. Much of the problem in our nation today with college graduates entering the workforce and demanding personal entitlements, we believe, stems from continuous bribes and rewards for completing assignments and/or simply behaving as expected.

A MODEL FOR IMPROVING INSTRUCTION AND BEHAVIOR

The thinking of humanist psychologists Abraham Maslow and Mortimer Adler, and cognitive developmentalists such as Erik Erikson, Richard Havinghurst, Lawrence Kolberg, and Jean Piaget, underlies The RCM Plan™. Based on this foundation, RCM shares some of the integrated ideas with the programs of Dreikurs, Nelson, and Glasser, but in a more practical and individualized manner.

RCM is based on the notion that every student moves through several common developmental stages. These stages determine, to a high degree, the behaviors, attitudes, cognitive capabilities, and physical characteristics that a student exhibits at any particular time. These proclivities, in combination with interactions with parents, siblings, peers, and teachers, greatly influence the pattern of behavior that a student adopts. To assure that students grow and prosper, and develop into healthy and well-balanced adults, every student needs unconditional love, security, and the certainty of belonging.

The ability to find workable solutions to life's problems is fundamental to a student's well-being. Within a hierarchy of learned behavior, the RCM model helps develop a capacity to solve problems. Students must be taught to examine and solve the many social and academic problems they will encounter during their growth. Accordingly, they must be given the opportunity to creatively and independently explore the world, define and achieve goals, and feel success upon which they will build self-assuredness, self-esteem, and ultimately, a strong self-concept.

RCM assumes that competent and responsible adults can teach most students, even so-called "problem" students and regardless of a student's socioeconomic or family history, to behave responsibly in the classroom, in school, and in the community at large. Behaving responsibly, according to RCM, means, in part, acting in accordance with an internalized set of values and beliefs, and with acceptance of the consequences of an act, whether positive or negative. On a continuum conveying degrees of responsible behavior, more responsible students self-correct behavior, use an internal locus of control, accept the consequences of their behavior, and follow guidelines to a greater degree than students who are less responsible. But regardless of where students fall on the continuum, most students can learn to behave responsibly. The real challenge lies in dealing with those few students—less than 5 percent of most classrooms—who exhibit anger, aggression, and mistrust in their behavior and attitudes. Their noncompliant behavior can be highly disruptive, and require exceptional treatment to make the classroom a viable operation. The RCM program addresses the needs of many of these students with the **intensive care unit** (a therapeutic removal from class, isolation, and counseling) and the team-led **discipline review committee**, both to be discussed later in this chapter. These tools use direct parent contact and establish two levels of contracts, **behavioral improvement agreements**, to include behaviors not responding to the previous plans. These tools function with appropriate consequences ranging from isolation, suspension, expulsion, and even entry into the juvenile justice system.

The Functions of the Discipline Review Committee

Classroom teachers use the intensive care unit (ICU) as a major consequence for significant disruptive classroom behavior, or intentional disrespect to a teacher or school employee. Students are removed from the setting where the offense has occurred and admitted to ICU. No work is permitted and the student must sit quietly and reflect upon the undesirable behavior. After the first visit to the ICU, the teacher meets with the student to establish procedures for avoiding a return to the ICU. Most students never return for a second visit. The discipline review committee (DRC), including parents and school administrators, monitors any rare second or third visits. No student is sent for a fourth time to ICU. Instead, a more severe consequence occurs. Usually by this time, the school is dealing with the top ten or so offenders in the entire school.

The DRC members, appointed by the principal or elected by the faculty, supervise all stages of The RCM Plan™. The DRC approves the overall school standard and guidelines, as recommended by the faculty and staff, and the chair serves as the major contact between teachers, students, and parents required to attend an ICU meeting. For each set of guidelines—such as behavior in the hall, parking lot, cafeteria, and other locations—a *specific* consequence correlates with the violation, including procedures for staff to follow. Prior to implementation or modification, the DRC must present the school's plan to the administration, faculty, and staff.

In the next step, individual teachers at the various grade levels and in special areas establish (or use the three we suggest) classroom guidelines (based upon school standards) and a pool of logical consequences for the classroom. After the first year, the faculty might seek student input as appropriate for revisions. This input allows students to be more involved in decision making and models participatory citizenship. Once the classroom plans are added to the school plan, the administration and staff establish an intensive care unit, prepare space, and develop a supervisory schedule. Two personnel are recommended to supervise the ICU at all times. The role of the DRC will be discussed in more detail in Chapter 4.

The ability to find workable solutions to life's problems is fundamental to a student's well-being. Within a hierarchy of learned behavior, the RCM model supports this capacity to solve problems. Students must learn to examine and solve the many social and academic problems that they will encounter during their growth. Accordingly, they must have the opportunity to creatively and independently explore the world, define and achieve goals, and experience success. Upon this, they will build self-assuredness, self-esteem, and, ultimately, a strong self-concept.

AN INVITATION TO CHANGE:
THE RCM PLAN™ INVENTORY

Before beginning the RCM approach to schoolwide classroom management, reflecting on beliefs about students, teaching, and learning will help clarify one's professional knowledge and attitudes about the underlying principles of RCM. The RCM Plan™ inventory assists in this process, and requires a simple response from "agree" to "disagree," with "uncertain" gauging an uncommitted response.

Once the inventory is complete, compare your results to the "ideal responses" we suggest. Strong general agreement on the items suggests an understanding and compliance with the fundamental principles and practices of RCM. A strong general disagreement signals either misunderstanding or rejection of RCM principles. Uncertain responses indicate a lack of clarity surrounding RCM, the meaning of a particular statement, or one's own values and practices. This is a crucial step because potential users must understand and agree with the driving principles of RCM for it to be successfully implemented. By examining responses, you can identify areas of concern and further explore the underpinnings of RCM before proceeding.

If you don't feel prepared to take the inventory at this time, revisit it after you finish other chapters or the entire book. Use the inventory individually or use it with the entire faculty for training, keeping in mind that it is not just an inventory—it is a teaching tool.

The RCM Plan™ Inventory

Item	Rating		
	Agree	Uncertain	Disagree
1. Students and adults move through common developmental stages that affect their behavior.			
2. Teachers should ignore student misbehaviors and smile or wink when acceptable behavior is observed.			
3. Students should be taught problem-solving methods.			
4. Self-assuredness, self-esteem, and a strong self-concept are fundamental to success in school.			
5. "Problem" or "dysfunctional" students cannot learn responsibility and should be separated from "normal" students.			
6. A poor socioeconomic and family history make it impossible for a student to learn responsible behavior.			
7. Students should rely on extrinsic motivation to control their behavior.			
8. Teachers should reinforce acceptable student behavior with items exchangeable for privileges, fun activities, and events.			
9. Responsible students self-correct their behavior, use an internal locus of control, and accept the consequences of their behavior.			
10. Teachers should reward a student immediately and frequently, especially at the beginning when the student is becoming familiar with correct behavior.			
11. Only a small number of students in almost any classroom require serious attention for misbehavior.			
12. Teachers should model appropriate values and behavior.			
13. Teachers should use positive and negative reinforcements to modify the behavior of students within the classroom environment.			

Item	Rating		
	Agree	*Uncertain*	*Disagree*
14. Teachers should carefully monitor their own behavior in the classroom.			
15. Teachers should avoid correcting a misbehaving student to prevent damage to the student's self-esteem.			
16. When a student expresses dismay for being denied satisfaction of a demand, teachers should change their own behavior to meet the needs of the student.			
17. Teachers' guidance precludes students from experiencing the consequences of their behavior.			
18. Students should be allowed to experience the natural consequences of their behavior.			
19. An authoritarian approach to discipline permits a student to develop an internal locus of control.			
20. Teachers should not be concerned with developing democratic and multicultural values.			
21. Human equality, dignity, self-worth, and participation in decision making at all levels should be taught by teachers and integrated into the curriculum.			
22. The school and classroom environment are not important for developing a responsible student.			
23. A safe and inviting classroom is irrelevant to a student's success in school.			
24. Teachers should clearly state the objectives of their instruction.			
25. Teachers should praise students for exceptional performance.			
26. Teachers should not punish a student for misbehavior.			
27. Punishment and consequences are not the same.			

(Continued)

(Continued)

Item	Rating		
	Agree	Uncertain	Disagree
28. Encouragement and praise will have the same positive effects on a student's attitudes and behavior.			
29. A responsible student relies solely on external rewards to motivate learning.			
30. External rewards are essential tools in controlling student behavior.			
31. Teachers should not rely on strict rules to control a student's behavior.			
32. Expressing strong emotions when dealing with a student's classroom misbehavior effectively controls that behavior.			
33. Teachers should closely monitor students for conformance to a code of discipline.			
34. Students should be involved in the development of behavioral standards and guidelines.			
35. Teachers should eliminate negative consequences so that a student enjoys school.			
36. Students should question the rules established by the teacher or school.			
37. Within the context of the classroom, students should not be expected to derive solutions to problems based on their rational understanding of their inner selves.			
38. Responsible behavior must be constantly reinforced with external inducements.			
39. A responsible student has internalized acceptable standards of behavior.			
40. Forcing a student to behave allows the student to internalize acceptable standards of behavior.			
41. A student is usually unwilling to cooperate unless forced to do so.			

Item	Rating		
	Agree	*Uncertain*	*Disagree*
42. Students should take an active role in developing and implementing learning experiences in the classroom.			
43. The rational, inner self is a myth.			
44. Students should be taught to act autonomously.			
45. A teacher's demeanor has substantial effects on a student's behavior in the classroom.			
46. Teachers should not use popcorn, candy, or other enjoyable items to positively reinforce an appropriate behavior.			
47. Students should be permitted to experience the consequences of their behavior.			
48. Teachers should arrange rewards to increase acceptable behavior.			
49. When students are treated equally, they are always treated fairly.			
50. Teachers should reward desirable behavior often and lessen the rewards as the desirable behavior is expressed.			
51. Students require a sense of security and belonging to function in school effectively.			
52. Due to misbehavior, students must sometimes be physically removed from the classroom environment and placed in a time-out area.			
53. To control behavior, teachers should direct a student to repeat an unacceptable behavior until the student is unwilling to continue doing so.			
54. Teachers should provide incremental rewards for small and incremental improvements in behavior.			
55. Most students do not require strong disciplinary actions in the classroom.			

Key to The RCM Plan™ Inventory

Agree: 1, 3, 4, 9, 11, 12, 14, 18, 21, 24, 26, 27, 31, 34, 36, 39, 42, 44, 45, 46, 47, 51, 52, and 55.

Disagree: 2, 5, 6, 7, 8, 10, 13, 15, 16, 17, 19, 20, 22, 23, 25, 28, 29, 30, 32, 33, 35, 37, 38, 40, 41, 43, 48, 49, 50, 53, and 54.

LOOKING AHEAD

Chapter 6 presented a scenario similar to the real-life classrooms teachers must face daily, followed by a description of the traditional classroom plans that focus on external-control models, such as fears or bribes, in comparison to The RCM Plan™—a well-tested, internal-control model that allows students to correct undesirable behaviors. From here, the various roles and functions of the discipline review committee (DRC) were explained. The next chapter presents procedures for setting up the instructional and classroom management environment.

7 Harnessing and Channeling Anger Into Constructive Outlets

Marilyn E. Gootman

Anyone can become angry. That's easy. But to be angry at the right person to the right degree at the right time for the right purpose and in the right way, that is not easy.

—Aristotle

Anger can create an unpleasant, tense undercurrent in the classroom. Angry students physically lash out at others, utter cruel and harsh words, and deliberately provoke their classmates and us. Teaching students how to manage and harness their anger is crucial for preventing some discipline problems and for maintaining a caring classroom community.

Defusing Student Anger on the Spot

Sometimes we need to take immediate action to defuse a student's anger before that student does something hurtful to himself or herself or to others. But trying to squelch anger by threatening a punishment if the student doesn't calm down or by just telling the student not to be angry probably will exacerbate the problem. Instead, I have found the following approach to be incredibly successful.

Acknowledge the Anger

Sometimes just acknowledging a student's feelings and his or her right to have these feelings is enough to resolve the problem. Don't we all need to vent at times? Just getting our feelings out of our system can be so therapeutic. All we want is someone to acknowledge our right to feel the way we feel. Acknowledging and validating a student's feelings can be challenging. What they see as an injustice may not appear that way to us. But they can't move on until we acknowledge their feelings in a nonjudgmental way. Listening with empathy does not mean that we agree with them (DiGiuseppe & Tafrate, 2007).

Let's see what happens in these two scenarios:

Kara crumples up her paper, throws it in the trash, and stomps back to her seat.

Ms. Lucas: What's that all about?

Kara: Nothing.

Ms. Lucas: Well, if it's nothing, young lady, take that paper out of the basket and continue writing on it.

Kara pouts during the rest of the lesson and gets no work done.

Ms. Lucas: Well, it's your choice, Kara. If you don't do the work, you'll have to miss recess today and make up your work.

Now, let's look at the same scene with the teacher listening and acknowledging Kara's anger:

Kara crumples up her paper, throws it in the trash, and stomps back to her seat. Ms. Lucas goes over to Kara's desk.

Ms. Lucas: Kara, that upset you. Apparently the paper displeased you.

Kara: Yes, it did. My pencil tip broke, and it made my paper look all messy.

Ms. Lucas: It sounds like you must have been embarrassed by how it looked.

Kara: Yes, I was. But I'll start another one now.

It didn't take any more time for the teacher to acknowledge how Kara was feeling, but it sure saved them both a lot of aggravation. The teacher–student rapport was improved, and both teacher and student saved face.

Helpful Tips for Acknowledging Anger

- Stay calm. Don't take their anger personally. Being frightened or wounded by a student's anger gives the student too much power. Be careful not to misinterpret or overreact to cultural differences in the expression of anger. If a teacher comes from a culture where anger is expressed indirectly, she may overreact to a child whose culture dictates "Say up front what's on your mind." Stay calm and don't get defensive.
- Allow them to express their feelings rather than trying to change them: "So you're feeling hurt" rather than "Come on, you don't really feel that way."
- Accept their feelings without arguing about their reasoning: "So you feel that . . ." rather than "You don't have a right to feel that way because . . ." or "You shouldn't feel hurt because . . ." Accept their feelings nonjudgmentally.

Ask Guiding Questions

Although sometimes just allowing a student to vent and express his or her feelings is enough to resolve the situation, at other times we can use our listening skills to help guide our students to figure out solutions to the problem that infuriated them in the first place. Our listening can become more active. After reflecting their feelings back to them and letting them know that we hear them, we can ask guiding questions. For example, "What seems to be the problem?" "What do you think you can do about it?" "Which solution do you think would work best?" This problem-solving approach is discussed in greater detail in Chapter 8.

Consider a situation in which the students have just come in from recess:

Mr. Powell: Please sit down and begin writing in your folder.

Several students are still wandering around the room.

Mr. Powell: If you are not seated by the time I count to 10, you'll have to sit out the last 5 minutes of the next recess so you'll be settled down by the time you return to class.

Latanya is still standing by her desk at the count of 10.

Mr. Powell: Latanya, you owe me 5 minutes at the next recess.

Latanya: But that's not fair!

Latanya slouches in her desk, pouting, fuming.

Mr. Powell: I gave you fair warning. You have no right to be angry. Just settle down and get to work.

Latanya mumbles several foul words under her breath and doesn't write one single word in her writing folder. The next round of the Latanya–Mr. Powell bout is about to begin.

Trying to stifle Latanya's anger created an even greater discipline problem. Let's look at how Mr. Powell could have defused this situation by giving Latanya a voice:

Mr. Powell: Latanya, next recess, you need to make up the time you wasted.

Latanya: But that's not fair!

Latanya slouches in her desk, pouting, fuming. Mr. Powell goes over to Latanya's desk and crouches down.

Mr. Powell: I can see that you're upset.

Latanya: I didn't do anything wrong. I always stand when I get out my writing folder.

Mr. Powell: Did you not have enough time to get out the folder?

Latanya: No, it takes me a while.

Mr. Powell: I wonder why you feel it takes you longer than anyone else.

Latanya: I guess because I was talking to Kay while I did it.

Mr. Powell: How do you think you could help yourself to do it faster next time?

Latanya: I'll tell Kay I can't talk until I get my folder out.

Did Mr. Powell agree with Latanya? Of course not. Many times, students' anger may seem unjustified or even silly to us. It would be absurd to agree with them. Sometimes, all we have to do is give them a sounding board so that they can get the anger out of their system and then guide them to solving their problem.

In the case of a raging, out-of-control child, acknowledging anger and asking guiding questions may be impossible. In that case, we can use our body language to help calm the situation. The key is not to assume a threatening demeanor. Here are a few suggestions:

- Keep our hands visible so that the child doesn't fear what's behind our backs.
- Assume a nonthreatening posture by keeping our hands unfolded with our palms visible.
- Respect the child's personal space by keeping a reasonable distance, up to 3 feet, to minimize his or her fear of us.
- Avoid a staring match so that no one assumes a combative stance.
- Try not to appear overpowering. Stoop or sit down if necessary to be at the child's level.
- Unless we must physically restrain a child to prevent that child from hurting himself or herself or from hurting someone else, avoiding physical contact works best in these situations. If we have to touch the child, the shoulder and the wrist would be the most effective places (Polowy, 1992).

Helping Students Harness Anger

We have just discussed how to deal with angry outbursts on the spot. Now let's explore how we can minimize them. All people get angry at times. Anger, like happiness and sadness, is a normal human emotion. People cannot control their feelings of anger any more than they can control their feelings of happiness, joy, sadness, or frustration. Feelings just are. Anger is neither a good nor a bad thing. What is "good" or "bad" is the way we handle the anger we feel (Prothrow-Stith & Weissman, 1993). Everyone, including our students, is entitled to angry feelings just as they are entitled to other feelings. But no one, including our students, is entitled to angry actions, such as lashing out at others verbally or physically. Let's explore how we can help students learn in three steps how to express and channel their anger constructively and nonhurtfully by teaching them anger-harnessing skills.

Psychologist Haim Ginott once said that just as the time to teach someone how to swim is not when that person is drowning, the time to teach someone how to harness his or her anger is not when that person is raging mad. It's most helpful to pick a quiet time to introduce some of these steps and directly teach the steps. We can also weave these skills into daily living and integrate them into our curriculum.

Step 1: Awareness

Self-Awareness

Someone bumps into Andy, he gets infuriated and lashes out with his hand. Lisa shoots out a whole litany of cuss words when she feels she has been wronged. Rella throws things when she gets angry. In order for these children to change what they are doing and to learn how to express their anger in an alternative fashion, they need to become aware of when they feel rage coming on so that they can catch themselves before they "lose it." Just as we can teach diabetic children to read their bodies' signals to detect the onset of insulin shock, so too can we teach students to read their bodies' signals to detect the onset of an anger outburst.

Our bodies have extraordinary ways of letting us know when we are angry and are about to lose control. Tensed muscles, grinding teeth, clenched fists, flushing in the face, goose bumps, shakiness, shivering, twitching, sweating, changing body temperature (hot or cold), laughing, crying, and stony silence are among the ways that our bodies signal anger. When students learn to identify their own anger signals, they can begin to detect that angry feeling before it overtakes them. They can stop and think before they act.

Many academic subjects can serve as excellent vehicles for heightening the awareness of the negative effects of angry feelings on our bodies and our actions.

> *Literature:* Discussions could include questions such as these: "How do you think the character looked when he was angry?" "What's the description of his face?" "Describe what you think his body felt like." "Think about a time when you felt that way." "Think about what your body felt like." "How do you think you look when you're angry?" "How can you tell when you're about to get angry?" Also, books such as Judith Viorst's *Alexander and the Terrible, Horrible, No Good Very Bad Day,* Judy Blume's books, and the Harry Potter series are excellent takeoff points for a discussion of anger and other feelings.
>
> *Writing:* Writing about their personal experiences of anger, such as what makes them angry, their maddest moment, or their pet peeve, can help students improve their writing and deal with people more

appropriately. Of course, they may choose not to share this writing with the class.

Social studies: Exploring expressions of anger among different peoples can be instructive for students. Some cultures discourage outward expressions of anger, whereas others encourage letting it all hang out. World events can be discussed in terms of anger, such as how anger often leads to war.

Transition times: Activities such as playing charades, taking photographs, and making faces in mirrors can heighten children's awareness of their bodily responses and are great transition time fillers.

These curricular activities can help students identify their own anger signals and allow them to detect when they are about to fly off the handle and then stop themselves from doing something that they will later regret.

Awareness of Others

In addition to not being able to catch themselves before they lash out in anger, many of our most troublesome discipline problems arise because children misread each other: "You looked like you were going to hit me." "I could see that you were angry at me." "Don't you diss me." Many times, students perceive slights when none are intended. They imagine peers to be more hostile than they are and interpret neutral situations as being threatening (Lochman, Dunn, & Klimes-Dougan, 1993). That is why learning how to read other people is important. The same kinds of activities that work for self-awareness will also work for awareness of others. Students can learn how to look, stop, assess the situation, and think before they react.

Step 2: Collecting Themselves

This step is designed to help students de-escalate. Angry feelings and actions can escalate and intensify quite rapidly. Anger feeds on itself, and unchecked anger snowballs. That's why it is so important to help our students become calm. But what happens when someone tells you to calm down when you're angry? Usually, it just makes you angrier. "Why should I calm down? I have a right to be angry." "Don't tell me what to do." Rather than tell our students to calm down, we can guide them to specific strategies that they can use to collect themselves:

Physical exercise: Exercise can help eliminate tension. Once the exercise stops, the body rebounds to a low arousal level. Jumping jacks, jumping rope, running around the track, and working out are all great releases. Of course, this kind of exercise isn't feasible in the middle of a lesson, but there are other times when it may be possible.

Separation: Sometimes it helps just to get away from the anger-provoking situation for a few minutes. Many teachers have found it helpful to have a time-out corner where children can go to collect themselves. This kind of time-out is designed to give students an opportunity to collect their thoughts, take a break from a heated situation, and calm themselves down. We can let our students know that it is designed as an aid in anger management and not as a punishment for anger. Punishing students for feelings, including anger, will only make students more angry, hostile, and resentful.

Distraction: Listening to music, reading, drawing, scribbling, or writing can prevent anger from snowballing. Attention is diverted away from the anger, and the activities themselves are calming. These activities can take place in the time-out corner.

Soothing activities: Deep breathing and counting backward from 10 are convenient ways for children to collect themselves in the classroom. All of our students, not just the very angry ones, could benefit from learning these techniques. The gentle back and forth of a rocking chair can extinguish the flames of anger, as can hugging a stuffed animal (even for upper elementary students).

Constructive activities: Building or making something can be helpful to some children. Manipulatives that keep their hands busy can be an excellent distracter. Twisting and turning something concrete like clay can release negative energy. Clay and some building materials can be placed in the time-out corner.

A note of caution: It's best to avoid suggesting punching pillows, spitting out angry thoughts, or screaming as techniques for the calming-down stage. Some maintain that these approaches help children get it out of their system. But current brain research advises against techniques that pump up the emotional brain's arousal because they leave the person even more angry (Tice & Baumeister, 1993). Our goal is to get the student calm enough to be able to verbalize his or her anger in a rational way.

Step 3: Talking and Labeling Their Feelings

This step teaches students how to constructively express anger. Once the student has cooled down, he or she should have the clarity of mind to be able to put his or her feelings into words and try to resolve the situation: "I was afraid that I might do it wrong." "I was embarrassed when they made fun of me." "I felt I deserved the sticker, not him." Through reflective listening, we can draw out their feelings and guide them to label the primary feelings that lie below the surface of anger—perhaps jealousy, nervousness, loneliness, discouragement, disappointment, embarrassment, fear, worry, humiliation, or sadness (see Chapter 5).

Anger is often a blanket that covers up many other feelings. What lies below the fury of the child who rips up his or her paper because he or she made a mistake? Fear of failure. What is the child feeling who lashes out after being teased? Embarrassment. Helplessness. Why is the student steaming because the field trip is canceled? Disappointment. Through reflective listening, we can guide the angry child to these insights: "It sounds like you were afraid that if you made mistakes you wouldn't pass" or "You sure seemed disappointed when we couldn't go on the field trip."

Summary: Harnessing Anger

We can expect that anger will surface in our classrooms. We can also expect this anger to be a loose cannon unless we help students learn how to deal with it constructively:

- Recognize the signs of anger in themselves and in others.
- Develop techniques for collecting themselves and de-escalating their feelings.
- Verbalize in a nonhurtful manner the primary feelings that lie below their anger.

In so doing, we can prevent many potential discipline problems from occurring.

Preventing Student Anger

Feelings of powerlessness lie at the heart of much student anger. By understanding that, we can try to give our students feelings of empowerment in the classroom. In so doing, we can prevent some anger from erupting in the first place.

Understanding What Makes Students Angry

Some children are angry the moment they enter our classrooms. We can practically see the steam rising. Their anger may have nothing whatsoever to do with us or their classmates but rather stems from their helplessness and powerlessness in their lives beyond the classroom. Anger shields them against feeling powerless in a situation where they feel threatened. A sense of endangerment, whether it be an actual physical threat or a symbolic threat to one's self-esteem, is a universal trigger for anger (Zillman, 1993).

Child Abuse

Many abused children fester with rage. Isn't anger a normal and, in fact, a healthy response to being deliberately hurt by someone else? But how can abused children possibly express their anger at those who mistreat them? They would risk even further mistreatment. So they submerge their anger into cauldrons boiling deep within them, venting steam on "safe" targets: other students and us.

Societal Rage

Class and race discrimination have hindered many groups from achieving success. Some children have had drilled into them the belief that the deck is stacked against them. Many seem perpetually irritable. They are sure that "the system," including teachers, has it in for them and that they have no hope (Prothrow-Stith & Weissman, 1993). They, too, feel powerless and inadequate.

Trauma

Many children have suffered from major traumatic losses, such as losing a parent or sibling, witnessing violence, or being in an accident. Anger is a common initial response to traumatic loss because the victim is totally helpless to prevent the tragedy.

Normal Living

Even children who do not have all this baggage often react with anger when they feel helpless—when they fear failure, when they are humiliated by put-downs or ridicule, when they think they have been treated unjustly by another, when they suspect dishonesty, or when they are not allowed to express their feelings. Some are supersensitive and overreact to any feedback or criticism. Most people, adults and children alike, respond with anger when they feel they have been robbed of their power.

Empowering Students

Because powerlessness or helplessness lies at the root of much of our students' anger, let's explore how we can structure our classroom to empower them. By designing positive sources of power for students and by trying to avoid situations where students feel powerless, we can both dramatically reduce the likelihood of triggering angry responses in students who are encumbered by extra baggage and avoid many of the daily hassles and annoyances that occur with all our students. Let's explore some positive sources of power.

Choice

By giving students choices among acceptable options, we can maintain our control and give them a sense of power and control as well. They have a choice, but only from the options we choose. We define the parameters. What are some empowering choices students can make while still meeting our objectives?

- The order in which they do their morning seatwork or other work or which book to read from a list of suggested books
- What to write about, given some guidelines or general parameters, or whom to sit with at lunch
- Which of several field trips they would like to take
- Which of several suggested topics they would like to study and in which order
- Which community service project they would like to adopt
- Which medium they choose for their artwork
- How they present their understanding of a topic in their project (straightforward oral reports, songs, poems, plays, videos, or visual displays)

Voice

Giving students a voice in the classroom, valuing what they have to say, is another tool for empowering them and thus for preventing anger from erupting. Penny Oldfather has coined the term *honored voice*. By listening to our students and caring about what they have to say, we help honor their voices (Oldfather, 1993; Oldfather & Thomas, 1999). When we don't care about what students have to say, they feel dishonored or disrespected ("dissed," in their language). And what happens when students are dissed? They lash out in anger. Why? Because anger is the power they use to defend their wounded egos. Schools of hope are places where children are honored (Kohn, 1998).

Does giving students a voice mean that they have the final say? Not at all. Rather, it means that we are willing to take their ideas into consideration:

- We will reflect about how we can incorporate subjects that are of interest to them.
- We will read their writings and respond thoughtfully.
- We will be sensitive to their expressions of feelings, be they positive or negative.

Yes, we'll honor their voices and listen to their ideas, but we teachers will still make the final decisions in the classroom.

Responsibility

One of the greatest power tools we can give our students is responsibility. In her research on people who had suffered abuse as children, Zimrin (1986) examined the characteristics of those who had grown up to live normal lives and those who had dysfunctional adult lives. One of the critical variables Zimrin found was that most of the healthy survivors had to assume responsibilities during their childhood. Other major studies have confirmed that a strong sense of responsibility greatly enhances resilience (Werner & Smith, 2001). Responsibility gives people power in their lives. When we feel empowered, we are less likely to vent our rage destructively.

Required Helpfulness

Required helpfulness (Rachman, 1979) is a strategy that many teachers have found to be successful for rechanneling behavior. Seven-year-old Toni was brought kicking and screaming into Ms. Bernard's first-grade classroom: "I hate school. I want to go home. Let me out of this damn place!" Toni had already attended two other schools, where she had spent the bulk of her days in an isolated time-out room because of her violent outbursts, and she had been retained one year. Imagine the nightmare for Ms. Bernard, having to cope with this child and the rest of her students as well. Unfortunately, many of us have been placed in similar quandaries.

Ms. Bernard adopted a required helpfulness plan as one of her strategies for acclimating Toni to her classroom. She arranged to pick up Toni in the front of the building 10 minutes before the rest of the students entered the classroom. Together, they walked to the class and chatted. In the classroom, Ms. Bernard assigned Toni some small tasks, such as passing out paper, sharpening pencils, or erasing the board. Periodically during the day, she would also call on Toni for assistance. Toni felt needed and important—she felt empowered. This required helpfulness, coupled with Ms. Bernard's calm, caring approach, resulted in a miraculous behavior change for Toni within just a few weeks.

How can we send our worst discipline problems on errands? Who knows what trouble they'll get into outside the classroom? Yet these are the very children who might benefit the most by being given responsibility. We can try to pair a child with behavior problems with another child who might be able to keep him or her in line and have them run an errand together. Sometimes we can't let a child out of our sight. If this is the case, we can try to enlist that child's help in the classroom. Passing out paper and other supplies, sharpening pencils, feeding the class pet, erasing blackboards, collecting papers, stapling material, designing bulletin boards, and setting up work areas are just a few examples of classroom responsibilities.

Working with a child's strength can be transformative for some children. Justin was a major disruptive force in the classroom. He was constantly making distracting noises that imitated bodily functions, inciting other classmates to act up, and picking fights in the playground. He seemed to have a chip on his shoulder. One day, Justin's science class began studying the sea. His eyes lit up. He was fascinated with fish and had read as many books as he could about them. He had even researched fish on the Internet and had communicated with a marine biologist. Justin's teacher seized this interest as an opportunity to enlist his required helpfulness. She asked Justin to prepare a lesson for the class and to be the resident expert to whom his classmates could come if they wanted some information about the sea. She also brought in an aquarium for the class and placed Justin in charge of maintenance and feeding. Soon, other teachers called on Justin for advice about their class fish. Justin no longer had the time or the need to attract negative attention.

Peer helper programs can also assist in transforming children's behavior by making the students feel needed. When an older child is asked to tutor a younger child, a weak student to help an even weaker student, or a charismatic troublemaker to be the class leader, the positive sense of power they acquire steers them away from rageful misbehavior. Community service is another avenue for helping children feel positive power. Students who are channeling their energy into helping others are far less likely to vent anger in our classrooms.

Beware of Power Struggles

One surefire way to get everyone riled up is for teachers to get into a power struggle with students. As teachers, we feel that we need to be in control, yet, at the same time, our students are struggling to assert themselves and establish their own individual identity and status. If we back them up against the wall, they will lash back in anger, either at that moment or at a later time. If we give them no graceful way to back out of a situation and maintain their dignity, they will come out shooting.

Billy's talking was getting on his teacher's nerves. "Get out in the hall this minute," Billy's teacher decreed. Billy remained seated. "Get out now." Billy remained seated. "Get out now or I'll carry you out." Billy remained seated. The teacher tried to physically remove Billy, and Billy resisted and told his teacher to get his hands off him. All the children watched as the principal was called in to settle the ruckus. Who do you think lost?

Anger can be triggered by a sense of endangerment. If students feel trapped, if they feel there is no way to save face but to sacrifice their dignity and their image in front of others, they'll try to take control and lash back in anger. Although they may be punished, we will suffer as well. It's just not worth it. Instead, the teacher could have tried a variety of other approaches. Giving an I message in a firm tone might have helped: "I get distracted when there is noise in the room, and then it's hard for me to focus on what I am teaching"; "I am concerned when there is an undercurrent of talking; some children may not be able to hear"; or "I am worried that by talking, you may miss out on understanding this concept." Or the teacher could have directly said, "Billy, I realize that you may understand this already, but others don't, and the talking can distract them and me"; or "Billy, please stop the talking; it's distracting." The teacher could have placed the responsibility onto Billy: "Billy, the talking is distracting. How can you help yourself not to do it?" (see Chapter 8 for further discussion of this problem-solving approach) or "Billy, please choose a place to sit where you won't be tempted to talk, because it's distracting." All these approaches get the message across very clearly and firmly that the behavior must be stopped without getting entangled in a power struggle.

Harnessing Our Own Anger

We're Human Too

Teaching can certainly be stressful. Some students push us to our limits. Rare is the teacher who hasn't at one time or another felt like Mount Vesuvius about to erupt. But trying our best to keep our cool and learning to channel our anger constructively are critical for teaching our students to do the same.

If we model constructive expression of anger, our students are more likely to mirror our behavior. If a teacher is angry, students may misbehave, reflecting the teacher's feelings. For some children, we are the only positive model in their lives. If we don't show them that adults can express angry feelings constructively, then they may never see that this is possible. To calm a frightened child, we must first calm ourselves (Perry, 2006).

Sudden outbursts can trigger jumpiness and anxiety in all children. For children who come from chaotic homes, our explosions can create a physioneurosis response, which can manifest itself as hyperactive, disruptive, unruly behavior. In addition, children who are not used to outbursts and those who are overprotected in their homes can become terrified. Fear affects the brain and makes it hard for one to think (Noteboom, Barnholt, & Enoka, 2001). The reverse is true as well: People think better when they are in a good mood. All children need calm, physically and psychologically safe environments if they are to behave properly and learn.

I have yet to meet a teacher who didn't get angry sometimes. We're human too! We are entitled to our feelings, including anger, just as our students are entitled to theirs. If we want to succeed in teaching our students to express their anger constructively, then we have to do the same. One way they learn is by copying us. For some children, we are their only adult model for appropriate behavior.

Pressures

We teachers are pressured from all directions—administrators, legislators, parents, the community, and children. Who wouldn't get angry and feel put-upon and overwhelmed at times! In this context, even normal children's behavior can sometimes infuriate us. We lose our cool because everything seems to be imploding on us. There are tests to grade, meetings to attend, lessons to plan, parents to assuage, administrators to please—we don't even have time to go to the bathroom! I have heard that teachers make up the bulk of urologists' patients. Is it any wonder? There's never a dull moment. Just when we think we have a minute to ourselves, something crops up. Under these conditions, it is understandable how, at times, we may lose our patience with our students, even when they have committed minor infractions or are only acting like children. Their behavior may be the straw that breaks the camel's back.

Frustrations

Times have changed. We seem to have so many more children in our classrooms nowadays with emotional and behavioral problems and learning disabilities. Many of our students' abilities to concentrate on their studies have been compromised by violence (real life and simulated), child abuse and neglect, and family disintegration. With so much else on their minds, it's hard for these students to concentrate. Sometimes when we teach these children, we receive blank stares, so we rephrase ourselves, and we still receive blank stares. We try other methods, and we receive yet more blank stares. Sometimes it seems nearly impossible to break through. Such frustration! We have feelings of helplessness and failure: "Why can't I make them obey?" "Why do they get to me so much?"

It's no wonder we feel angry! Although it is not the children's fault, it's not ours either. We cannot possibly be psychologists, social workers, and educators at the same time. Just as with children, our feelings of helplessness and powerlessness can make us angry.

Daily Hassles

Normal children's behavior can be infuriating at times. Why? Sometimes their behavior makes us afraid. For example, when they try dangerous tricks on the playground, we get angry because we're frightened; that's our primary feeling. When they fight, we often feel helpless and worried about someone getting hurt, so we get angry. When we have a lot to do, deadlines to meet, and they move slowly, it raises our ire. When they daydream, it's annoying to have to repeat ourselves. Just because their behavior is normal doesn't mean it won't get on our nerves. And normal children will misbehave. It goes with the territory of being a child. But just as it is normal for them to make mistakes sometimes, it's normal for us to feel annoyed and angry when they do.

Baggage From Our Private Lives

"Mom, where does Mrs. Lumpkin sleep at night? There's no bed in the school." Despite what some kindergartners may think, we all have lives beyond the classroom with our own responsibilities, joys, and worries. When we get in an argument with a loved one or are anxious about someone's health, it's hard to leave our feelings at the schoolhouse door. At those times, we can send out a clear alert to our students: "I'm feeling a bit stressed out today, so tread carefully"; "I'm upset about something today; it has nothing to do with you, but I am extremely sensitive"; or "I would appreciate extra cooperation today; I am not feeling well." Not only do communications like these help us get through the day, they help our students develop empathy, a critical aspect of emotional intelligence.

Baggage From Our Past

Sometimes, our students' behavior triggers painful memories of our own problems in school. The old adage "sticks and stones can break my bones, but names can never harm me" is a big lie. Names can harm us and harm us deeply. Many of us still cringe at the mention of a name we were called in childhood. If we hear our students calling a student a hurtful name, we may explode: "Don't let me ever hear you call him a name again. How can you be so mean? If you say that again, I'll punish you. How would you like it if we called you that?" Our overreaction might very well make matters worse for the name-calling victim; now they might be called "teacher's pet" or "baby." We should try to stop the name calling while keeping our cool. Sometimes we may feel that our students are getting away with things that we never got away with. We may feel resentful and even a bit jealous.

We also bring our own cultural baggage with us. Behaviors that are perfectly normal in another culture may be foreign to us and even offensive. We may be furious when a child does not look at us when we are talking to him or her because to us that seems disrespectful. However, in some cultures it is considered disrespectful for a child to look an adult in the eye.

When we overreact, we can try to do some self-analysis: Why does this upset me so much? Does this remind me of something way back in my own childhood? We can try to remind ourselves, "Now is different. I am no longer a child. These children are not my family or my peers." Some teachers find it helpful to talk these kinds of situations through with a trusted colleague who isn't emotionally entangled. Understanding and then setting this childhood baggage aside can help us to stay calm during challenging discipline situations.

Harnessing Our Anger

Angry feelings in themselves aren't bad. It all depends on what one does with them. When expressed constructively and nonhurtfully, anger can be a terrific motivator for effecting change. Let's look at how we can harness our anger to effect positive change in our classrooms.

Step 1: Notice Our Body's Message

"I was burning mad." "I was so angry my heart was beating a mile a minute." "I was so angry I felt like crying." "Every time I get angry I grind my teeth." Our bodies have marvelous ways of letting us know when we are angry and about to "lose it": feeling hot or cold, muscle tension, fist clenching, teeth grinding, sweating, laughing, crying, heart beating fast, head hurting, body shaking or shivering, body stiffness, twitching, or just frozen silence. By listening to our body's message, we can become aware of our rising anger and can harness it before it reaches a crescendo and gets out of control.

Step 2: Collect Ourselves

Once we hear our body signaling that we are about to lose it, we can try to collect ourselves. It is okay to let our students know that that's what we're doing:

- Remove ourselves from the situation if possible. Perhaps we can stand in the hall by the door for a few minutes or call on a paraprofessional to take over for a short time. One teacher of young children sits in the rocking chair in her classroom, which she calls the "power chair." She tells the students that she's upset and needs to rock for a few minutes to collect herself. Not only does this help the teacher with her immediate problem, but it also models this behavior for her students.
- Do deep breathing, count to 10, count backward from 10, or use visual imagery. Sometimes we can do this even when we're in the midst of teaching. It is okay for students to know what we're doing; they'll see that we have feelings and that we're trying to express them constructively, and we hope they'll follow suit.
- Do something with our hands: Straighten the desk, write, or even put our hand up to our mouth to help us remember not to say anything we might later regret.
- Physical exercise is a tremendous release but isn't possible when we are in the middle of teaching. Have you noticed that exercising each day helps take the edge off things?

Step 3: Put It Into Words

Here's where an I message can help us express our feelings in nonhurtful ways while getting our students to change their behavior. Keep in mind that our tone of voice, as well as our words, conveys our message. We need to be firm and direct to get our message across. If we smile while we're telling a student we're angry about something, the student will get a mixed message. Let's review the steps in constructing an I message (discussed in Chapter 5) and see how we can use it as a discipline tool.

"When . . ." Without accusing, we can describe the behavior we want changed. Being specific about the "when" (what was going on) provides

students with clear information about what needs to be changed and how they can change it. It also encourages them to feel that they can indeed change and are not stuck in a rut. "You always . . ." or "You never . . ." imply that things are never going to change, whereas "Today . . ." or "I just noticed . . ." narrow it down to a manageable time frame.

It helps to limit ourselves to just this specific incident rather than bringing in all past infractions. If we stay focused on the issue at hand, students are less likely to tune us out like a broken record. What happens when we say, "If I've told you once, I've told you a hundred times . . ."? They roll their eyes and think, "There she goes again."

The key here is also not to put the student on the defensive by pointing a finger with an accusatory "you." "I feel put-upon when there are papers on the floor," rather than "You're such slobs"; or "I feel distracted when there's an undercurrent of noise," rather than "You're such noisy people." It's highly unlikely that they will heed our words if they feel they are under attack and on the defensive.

"I Feel . . ." Here's where we try to put the primary feeling that lies below the anger into words: worried, frustrated, hurt, overwhelmed, insulted, betrayed, frightened, disappointed, anxious, sad, concerned, or nervous. "I am worried that we will not finish our work if there are more interruptions." Students don't usually think about our feelings. In fact, they sometimes forget that we have any feelings. Some children are very sensitive when it comes to their own feelings but are not sensitive to the feelings of others. Here is yet another opportunity to develop their empathy for adults. And although our students may argue or disagree with our policies, they cannot argue with our feelings any more than we can argue with theirs. If we say, "I'm disappointed that you misbehaved when I was out of the room," they can't say, "No, you're not disappointed" or "No, you don't feel that way."

"Because . . ." This is when we explain why we feel this way, how their behavior tangibly and concretely affects us. We're not pulling our feelings out of thin air. We have a good reason for feeling that way. This sells our message because it justifies our right to our expectations. They see that it makes sense to expect the change: "I am concerned because we might not have enough time to play that kickball game today" or "I am irritated because I cannot concentrate." What goes through our students' minds when they hear us talk this way? Typically, they might think, "Gee, I had better hurry up so we can go out to play" or "I had better be quiet so the teacher can concentrate." Our "because" often causes them to stop and think about the ramifications of their actions and leaves the decision up to them.

Anger can motivate us to bring about change. By harnessing our anger and using I messages, we teachers can use our anger to solve and even prevent some discipline problems. I messages let students know how we feel, why we feel that way, and what they can do about it.

Summary of Main Points

- Both students and teachers are entitled to their angry feelings as well as a variety of other feelings.
- We can defuse student anger by acknowledging their feelings, getting students to verbalize them, and guiding them to solve the problem that triggered the anger.
- Students and teachers can learn how to harness their anger and express it constructively.
- Some anger can be defused in the classroom by providing students with positive sources of power.
- The first step in harnessing anger is identifying when we are angry or when others are angry.
- The second step in harnessing anger is developing our own strategies for collecting ourselves.
- The third step in harnessing anger is talking directly and constructively in a nonblaming way.

8

Avoid Win-Lose Power Strategies

Jane Bluestein

I possess tremendous power to make a child's life miserable or joyous. I can be a tool of torture or an instrument of inspiration. I can humiliate or humor, hurt or heal. In all situations, it is my response that decides whether a crisis will be escalated or de-escalated, and a child humanized or de-humanized.

Haim Ginott[1]

It is incongruous to expect children to be respectful when you are not respectful in your attitude toward them.

Mary Robinson Reynolds and Craig Reynolds[2]

We look forward to the time when the Power of Love will replace the Love of Power. Then will our world know the blessings of Peace.

William E. Gladstone[3]

You know when it takes three strong adults to remove a six-year-old from the classroom, something is wrong. This happened during my first week of student teaching in a first-grade class (which followed a successful and enjoyable stint in a sixth-grade class with students who, frankly, made much more sense to me). Whatever set this child off, I have no idea. I just remember that he was beyond anything anyone could do to calm him down. Teaching and learning had become impossible, and he had become a danger to himself and the other students. Out of the classroom, he settled a bit, but getting him there was another story.[4]

This is the kind of situation that throws everybody into survival mode—not exactly where we do our finest work. None of us in education enjoys encounters like these, and anyone who spends much time functioning in survival mode won't last long in the profession. There will always be factors in children's lives you won't know about or be able to control—conditions and events that impact them before they even walk into your room. So it's critical to create the structures, connections, and relationships to prevent these dramas from happening—or at least to reduce the frequency and intensity of incidents that occur.

BEHAVIOR MANAGEMENT AND TEACHER PREPARATION

If there is a particular arena in which a win-win approach will reap the most profound benefits, it is in the area of discipline, or what is often referred to as classroom management or behavior management. You would think, since this aspect of teaching is such a fundamental prerequisite to actual instruction and learning (which frankly won't happen in the absence of cooperative and attentive student behavior), that teacher-training programs would place a great premium on helping prospective teachers develop these skills. Yet the opposite seems to be true.

Of all the areas teachers identify as the ones in which they receive the least useful information and preparation, behavior management consistently tops the list. "The greatest area of need for new teachers is classroom management," wrote Mary Vaglica, an elementary assistant principal, mentor, and supervisor. "Teachers are never fully prepared for discipline issues that occur, [or for] managing the classroom so that students can work independently, and so the teacher can work with small groups." Former principal Lulu Lopez agreed. When asked what she saw as the greatest need for the beginning teachers she has observed in her forty-two years in education, she replied without a second's hesitation, "Behavior management." Few teachers would disagree. Over and over, contributors protested the lack of preparation for the realities they experienced in their classrooms. "I really wish somebody had told me that classroom management is your single biggest battle," said Darren Raichart. "Some people do tell you that in college, but then they spend most of your classes teaching you other things." Holly Davis shared, "I wish my education classes had dealt more with classroom management. I love my subject so finding new ways to teach and grow is easy, but there are still students who defy my most tried-and-true management strategies."

Wherever you work, you can count on having students who lack the self-management, social-interaction capabilities, and the learning behaviors that would otherwise free up your time for actual teaching. Unfortunately, the majority of resources that would attempt to help you deal with these shortcomings tend to be presented in outdated, ineffective, and very win-lose terms. And absent more positive alternatives, these are the strategies we tend to perpetuate because they're familiar and they're there. (And they are generally familiar to administrators and parents as well.) When they don't work, the strategies get repackaged or renamed, but in essence, we keep doing the same things over and over, even when they don't work, even when they make things worse.

Let's step back a bit and get some perspective on how we got to this place. "In previous generations within our lifetime, the values taught by the home, the school, and the media were basically in harmony," wrote author and educator Marvin Marshall. "The values taught outside the home were supportive of values in the home. Needless to say, that is not the situation today."[5] A few decades ago, the most serious complaints about students' behavior listed children who talked out, chewed gum, or ran in the hall. Subsequent generations of teachers have had to contend with these annoyances in addition to fighting, gang activity, and "problems of weapons, substance abuse, and violent assaults against other students and school staff."[6]

I can understand the hunger for the good old days, along with the discipline strategies that may have been effective in our recent and distant past. But many teachers have found that tried-and-true methods no longer hold the clout or effectiveness they once did. Some still clamor for the harsh penalties of the past, arguing for more of the strategies they idealize from their days as students—or from wistful stories they've heard—only invoked bigger and harder, and with the absurd notion that anything to the contrary is soft and permissive.

But nostalgia seldom accounts for the frequent failures—or the academic and emotional cost—of draconian authority, and it's easy to forget that there have always been opponents to the kind of strict discipline that many in and out of the profession would celebrate.[7] The problem seems to stem from the challenge in finding any win-win middle ground. "At some point in the history of education," wrote educators William Purkey and David Aspy, "a myth developed that education has to be either humane or effective, but that it is impossible to be both. The sad part about this myth is that it has been accepted as reality even though there is a wealth of data to refute it."[8] There is still a fair amount of black-and-white thinking regarding what is necessary to teach children to be civilized members of a school community and society in general, including an assumption that allowing students autonomy will undermine adult authority, or the equally stubborn notion that we have to hurt, criticize, embarrass, or otherwise discomfort students in some way in order to change their behavior. Despite efforts to address this issue in teacher-training and inservice programs, too many offerings are presented in this all-or-nothing, authoritarian context, capitalizing on the fear of kids being completely out of control unless the appropriate sanctions and penalties are in place. But far too many of these approaches are anachronistic and inappropriate to win-win intentions, and considering changes in the student population and culture in general, it's not surprising to hear how many teachers find these strategies to be ineffective and, in some cases, to actually create more problems than they solve.

We have some pretty big hurdles to clear if we're going to get past old win-lose mindsets, much less the discipline traditions still being recommended, used, and supported. I'm going to ask you to take the hard road here and reject the formulas, packages, and quick-fix approaches, as attractive and well supported as they may seem, in favor of developing relationships, questioning assumptions and traditions, and putting your faith in process over product. And rather than worrying about what to do when a student does something disruptive or inappropriate, let's look at what we can do to prevent these problems before they occur. Be assured that by creating a win-win community in your classroom, it is possible to minimize, if not eliminate, the discipline problems that happen when students are competing with adults for power, as well as those fermented in the students' social environment. Win-win solutions give us an open window or side-door access when the main entrance is blocked. But first let's take a look at some of the traditions that are cluttering our path.

OUR MOST BELOVED (AND PERSISTENT) WIN-LOSE TRADITIONS

Think about all the things that can impact students' behavior and attention—how a lesson is being taught, their interest in the subject, the relevance of the content, a comment or look from another student in the hall or on the playground, something that happened at home or in the community, how much sleep or nutrition they had before they came to school, the physical aspects of the classroom (furniture, lighting, arrangement, temperature, and even the color of the walls), the degree to which their biological needs (for movement, water, and bathroom breaks) are being met, or even the weather. Factor in teacher personalities and class dynamics, and it's understandable that any child might exhibit behaviors we deem undesirable, at least occasionally.

Dealing with student behaviors, whether quietly inattentive or disorderly and disruptive, has been one of the greatest challenges for teachers throughout history. Clearly, some responses are more effective than others, not just in their effect on subsequent student behaviors, but also on the climate of the class, their impact on other students, and their ability to support win-win objectives.

Let's look at some of the most common behavior-management strategies and assumptions you're likely to encounter and do some quick and dirty myth busting, examining why these approaches will run anywhere from pointless to counterproductive, often with a side of needless complication and hidden dangers.[9] You'll find constructive, win-win ideas in the following chapter, but get acquainted with these traditions first, because depending on where you're teaching, there's a good chance that you *will* encounter them and they will be held up as recommended protocols, which will add to the enticement to use them. But don't be fooled by familiarity, and know that these are the discipline approaches that have been adding stress to teachers' and students' lives forever. Don't say I didn't warn you.

Control

There's this overt expectation that teachers be in control of their classrooms, which many educators interpret to mean being in control of their students. Assuming that this were even possible, consider the innate need we *all* have for some autonomy and control in our lives. This is the need that makes even the most cooperative of us resentful and resistant to being pushed around or having others try to control us. For this reason, competition for control can turn into a rather ugly win-lose (or no-win) battle of wills. While the first grab for autonomy surfaces around age two, as kids get older, their ability and resources to prove "you can't make me" can get rather sophisticated and effective. If you can resist the urge to seek ways to out-power these students (and "win" at their expense), there are some side-door approaches that will allow them the autonomy they want within the limits you need. In other words, instead of looking for a better way to make them lose, let's start asking the magic, win-win question, "How can we all get what we want?"

"All modern experimental work points to how important for good health is the perception that an individual is in charge of his own destiny," reported researcher Michael S. Gazzaniga, reporting that efforts to undermine people's sense of power and control in their lives can lead to a great deal of stress, along with all kinds of compensating behaviors, or what some might call "acting out." (This can occur whether people are actually being controlled or whether they simply believe that they are unable to impact their own lives.)[10] But all-or-nothing thinking leads back to the win-lose notion that either we are in charge or *they* are. So before I go any further, please let me assure you that a win-win approach to power dynamics *is still an authority relationship*. You are still the boss and you still get to be in charge. You just accomplish this goal without needing to disempower anyone, and as a by-product, you get to avoid so many of the power struggles and other problems that tend to plague adults using authoritarian, win-lose power dynamics. (See "Negative Outcomes of Win-Lose Authority Relationships.")

This model is so common that many of us step up to the plate without even questioning the assumption that this is how we're supposed to be. John Taylor Gatto shared the disciplinary mindset so common in schools. "By stars and red checks, smiles and frowns, prizes, honors, and disgraces, I teach kids to surrender their will to the predestinated chain of command," he wrote. "Rights may be granted or withheld by any authority without appeal, because rights do not exist inside a school—not even the right of free speech, as the Supreme Court has ruled—unless school authorities say they do. As a schoolteacher, I intervene in many personal decisions, issuing a pass for those I deem legitimate and initiating a disciplinary confrontation for behavior that threatens my control."[11]

This kind of thinking would explain the tendency for schools and teachers to micromanage the minutiae of students' lives, from how they sit to what they wear, from when they can talk to how they can manage their biological needs for movement, hydration, or a bathroom break. And it would also explain the beliefs that drive much of the policing and punishing many teachers fear they need to adopt to keep the class from going to hell in a handbasket. But the more we try to monitor and control, the more kids have to fight against and the less their incentive to assume personal responsibility for their behavior or develop the self-control we say we desire. (And by the way, discipline programs that rely on surveillance cameras, metal detectors, and a police presence have an intensely negative impact on school climate and have also been shown to negatively affect graduation rates and rates of suspension.[12])

This approach also has a human cost and will invariably get in the way of learning for many students. Middle school teacher Bill Funkhouser shared, "It is almost painful to reflect on who I used to be. I was so caught up in getting students to obey that I lost sight of the humanity of this profession. I was overpowering them—rather than being flexible, understanding, and compassionate." Similarly, an offhand comment by one of his students made high school teacher John Keydash realize how much of his classroom management depended on fear. "It took awhile to learn that what I thought was the superlative of teacher management technique was only half there because I lacked the connection [with my students]," he wrote. "I needed to be understanding and caring but at the same time keep students responsible and accountable. I did not want to manage learning because my students were afraid of me." Besides, a well-controlled classroom is not the same as an actual self-managing one, and I've known teachers whose seemingly well-behaved kids went wild the moment the adults left the room or turned their back.

"How much superior an education based on free action and personal responsibility is to one relying on outward authority," proposed Albert Einstein.[13] And consider Ralph Nader's contention that "the function of leadership is to produce more leaders, not more followers."[14] If we're concerned about building independence and self-management, keep in mind that controlling kids does not grace them with the skills or the confidence to control themselves when no adults are around. There are many effective alternatives to establish the structure your kids will need to function successfully and cooperatively that put far less stress on your management system—and your nervous system as well.

Negative Outcomes of Win-Lose Authority Relationships

Win-lose power struggles are stressful for everyone in the room and especially frustrating, time-consuming, and exhausting for teachers. In addition, attempts to control kids can naturally trigger unwanted student reactions—whether defiance, resistance, shutting down, or giving up. Control reinforces dependence and helplessness and can erode confidence kids need to function and make decisions in the absence of adult guidance. Even apparently desirable compliant behavior presents its dangers in the difficulty these students have when it comes to resisting peer pressure or making decisions in their own best interest. (Compliant students often make decisions based on what they believe would gain someone's approval or protect against someone else's anger, rejection, humiliation, or abandonment. Or they do what they're told, so they can avoid any responsibility for the outcomes of their choices, which are always "somebody else's fault.") Let's help kids learn how to think, anticipate outcomes, and make positive choices, rather than continuing to insist that they simply do as they're told.

Coercion and Punishment

It's almost instinctive, with the upbringing and school experiences most people have had, to assume that something bad *has* to happen to children who have done something wrong, refused to do something they were asked to do, or addressed an adult in a tone deemed oppositional or disrespectful, for example. This pattern consistently shows up in school and district discipline codes, which invariably include a list of rules and violations, each with escalating penalties for infractions.

A little tangent here: You're going to hear these penalties or punishments referred to as "consequences," probably with an argument about them being logical in the context of the misbehavior. But logical or not, I'm betting that the consequence listed will be negative, rendering it punitive—in nature, energy, and intent. Even discipline codes and student manuals that attempt to include a positive focus by listing desirable behaviors still tend to rely heavily on the parts that admonish, "and here's what will happen if you *don't* do this." I understand the political need for these documents. I'm just asking us to quit expecting them to achieve the goals that relationships, structure, opportunities for decision making, positive outcomes, good follow-through, clear directions, and other win-win strategies can accomplish.

Back up and ask, "What's the point of these discipline codes?" What you'll most likely hear is a desire for respectful, cooperative student behavior.[15] But how effective is the fear of punishment when it comes to actually motivating positive behavior? "The object of punishment is prevention from evil," argued education reformer Horace Mann. "It never can be made impulsive to good."[16] The problem with depending on a hierarchy of increasingly negative consequences is that it relies on students' fear of punishment and often requires increasingly harsh outcomes to generate responses from students, which, incidentally, aren't always positive, especially when kids get to the point where they figure they don't have much left to lose. Marvin Marshall noted that "a prime reason—both for teachers leaving the profession and the concern for discipline—is the clinging to coercive approaches as a strategy for motivating students to behave appropriately. If coercion were effective in reducing inappropriate behavior, discipline problems in schools would be a footnote in history."[17]

And what if the student doesn't care? I've seen kids deliberately act up to get thrown out of a class they didn't like or dismiss detention as little more than a chance to get their homework done before they left school.[18] I've met kids with so many hours assigned to afterschool punishments that they would have been in their twenties before their entire sentence was served. And I've even observed little ones who shrug off a name on the board, a missed recess, or a call home. Now what? Are you willing to risk depending on a strategy that paints students into an adversarial corner and can easily escalate or backfire? "When students are not afraid, punishment loses its efficacy," Marshall added.[19]

Besides, it won't take long before you start to notice that it's nearly always the same kids whose names end up on the board or on detention slips, a testament to just how ineffective these classic sanctions are.[20] And if you imagine that a stronger punishment, like tossing a kid out on the street for really bad behavior, will teach cooperation, think again. Here's a little note about the human costs of disciplining by suspension and expulsion, courtesy of Jo Ann Freiberg, education consultant. "Nationally the rate of suspension and expulsion has doubled since the 1970s," she reported, the majority of them for "non-dangerous behaviors." She asks that we keep in mind that while kids are not in school, they are not able to benefit from a potential connection with their teachers, are not receiving academic instruction, and do not benefit from an intervention to ameliorate the behavior in question. Not surprisingly, increased suspension and expulsion correlates with lower test scores and an increased likelihood of these students engaging in risky behavior, dropping out, and becoming entangled in the justice system.[21] Not exactly the positive outcomes we say we're shooting for. And as far as promoting connectedness goes, harsh, restrictive school policies have the opposite effect, as reflected in a high prevalence of disconnected students at those sites.[22]

But even in the face of the well-documented failure and expense of a punitive approach, watch how hard it is to let go of these strategies. I've had avowed converts to a win-win philosophy who still insist on pulling colored warning cards or writing the names on the board—just in case. OK, so they're not there yet. But at some point, I will gently invite them to get off the fence and focus on more positive approaches. When they defend their strategies with a tired cliché about life being tough, I'll share a quote from author Carolyn Kenmore to point out the possibility of a totally different way to think about their authority relationships with students: "If you can learn from hard knocks, you can also learn from soft touches."[23]

Rules, Rules, and More Rules

There is so much mythology around the power of rules that it's easy to start believing that you won't need much else to establish your authority in the classroom. Rules are sacred cows in education that nobody seems to question much, possibly because to do so would suggest chaos and anarchy. Take note, though, that I'm not recommending a lack of structure, which we all need to function and feel safe. But the idea that we can counter misbehavior by making rules—much less that a lack of cooperation is rooted in a lack of *enough* rules—is utter nonsense.

"You cannot make rules based on the exception," said Littke and Grabelle.[24] Nonetheless, I see this tendency over and over again, adding new rules to discipline handbooks any time a student does something an adult doesn't like. Afraid of leaving any stone unturned, some lists include so many details about what kids shouldn't do, say, wear, or bring to school that the rules lose their meaning. (When I was working on a book for high school students, one of my favorite quotes came from a kid who urged, "Get rid of the stupid little rules. Whoever wrote in the handbook that we shouldn't bring ninja stars and swords to school is a moron."[25] Can you imagine this individual taking the rules—or the adults in that school—very seriously?)

I've noticed, too, that the number of rules in a classroom or school tends to correlate highly with the number of behavior problems there. Go figure. The problem is that while rules can provide a starting point for determining the kind of structure you want, they don't actually *inspire* kids to be cooperative and civilized. Besides, emphasize rules and you send a subtle message that your priority is policing and enforcing. Mahoney and Purr advised against starting off the year by "standing in front of the class and reading rules and regulations. This . . . gives the wrong impression. Kids don't want a list of all the things they are not allowed to do. You will look too authoritative and inflexible."[26]

Students behave because it pays off, not because there is a rule somewhere telling them to do so. They behave because in a caring, mutually respectful, win-win classroom, that's just how people act. (Sure, some will test the limits, and some will cooperate so they don't get in trouble, which is a payoff too—though generally the weakest enticement of the lot. Most will find the positive outcomes far more attractive.) I'm always touched by how willing some young people are to take responsibility for their own behavior when we give them a little credit and a bit of breathing room. I've seen students manage themselves quite effectively in classrooms in which the one and *only* rule instructed kids that they could do whatever they wanted as long as it didn't interfere with anyone's teaching or learning.[27]

So by all means, post the rules if you are required to do so. Just don't expect the list to do a thing besides protect the district and maybe impress some people who visit your classroom.[28] (And don't forget, because of the way the brain works, your kids will stop noticing it's even there after a couple of days.) I've never seen students restrain themselves from outbursts, disruptions, or other misbehaviors simply because the list of rules on the wall caught their eye before they had a chance to act out. The list may give you an artificial sense of power—after all, you've got something to point to when a child misbehaves—but the list will not make kids be good.

Consistency and Rigidity

I've never understood the importance my training accorded to consistency, perhaps because I never completely understood what people meant when they advised us to "be consistent." Over the years, I've come to suspect that they were hinting at the need to do what we say we're going to do, which for my money speaks more to the need for good follow-through than consistency. There is a difference, especially in terms of behavioral guidelines and motivation.

Although rules are often invoked in the name of fairness, the fact is, there is little uniformity in which rules are enforced from one classroom to another, or even from one child to another.[29] And the rules themselves can be a bit of a problem, because sometimes there just isn't enough time for students to get to their locker or stop at the bathroom between classes, sometimes they forget to silence their phone, and sometimes the dog does eat their homework. Am I suggesting that we start asking for excuses or become even more arbitrary? Of course not. However, I will argue for some flexibility *built into* the structure we create—before the problems or exceptions arise—and for the willingness to reconsider rules that don't support what actually works.

I recently received an e-mail from a middle school teacher who, among the accommodations he was willing to offer his students, allowed them to wear hats in class. Only a few students took advantage of the privilege—some due to light sensitivities, others perhaps to make a statement of personal style or comfort. Although the offer worked very well as a motivator for a couple of students and did not cause any particular problem in or out of the classroom, the superintendent decided to pull the plug. "The funny thing is, one student in particular, probably our toughest in terms of behavior, was an angel for the two weeks that he was permitted to wear a hat. Did all of his work, stayed focused. We really thought he turned a corner," he wrote. "Then, when [the superintendent] told us to enforce the no-hat rule, his behavior began to spiral out of control. Now, he hasn't done one assignment in a week, and gets kicked out of class probably two out of five classes per day." Here was a child "determined to do anything to not lose the privilege," who now had no incentive to do what anyone wanted.

Rather than get into a discussion of hats or no hats, the point here is that some kids require precious little to get them on board, and flat-out denying the things that work best for them (and their teachers) ends up, as it did here, in a no-win outcome. I've heard dozens of stories like this where, in stunning examples of what journalists Jerry Adler and Karen Springen called "a tremendous victory for bureaucracy over common sense,"[30] a no-drug policy is invoked to suspend a high school girl with Midol in her purse, a middle school boy is expelled for possession of a weapon he found and turned into the office, and a five-year-old is suspended for a day for wearing a fireman costume that included a plastic ax. Is it any wonder kids sometimes have a hard time reckoning with adult authority, much less respecting it?

Some of the most common "yeah, but" questions I get in my seminars refer to dealing with a crisis situation, particularly one in which a student goes over the edge. (Our win-lose programming can be pretty strong. Some people are willing to put only so much faith in the power of prevention, win-win power dynamics, and solid relationships with kids—your ace in the hole, by the way, when the rare crisis occurs in a win-win classroom.) So I looked at the literature and programs I could find and talked to a number of counselors and crisis intervention specialists, and I discovered a hodgepodge of advice: *Talk softly. Be loud and authoritative. Use humor. Avoid humor. Use physical proximity. Don't get too close. Send the child out of the room. Keep the child in the room, but send everyone else out to a predetermined location.* In other words, any strategy can work sometimes and so can its complete opposite. In addition, any strategy can backfire and make things worse. There are factors at work beyond what you can know or see, and most often, you're making a split-second judgment call, because different kids and different situations will call for different approaches. Trying to rely on a formulaic response can actually create more problems than it solves.

Let's pick our battles very carefully. There will be days when things the students do bother you a lot more than they normally might, so you will need to ask for certain behaviors you might not ordinarily require. And there will be rules that would have you bust kids for things you might never notice and don't care about, and rules that obstruct the very things that might help your students focus, attend, and self-manage.[31] There is no one way to respond to every student, every behavior, or every situation.

If you want to find a good use for consistency, commit yourself to being consistent in terms of following through on the conditions for positive outcomes you allow, modeling your behavior to reflect the way you would like your students to act, and holding on to your long-range goals and win-win ideals. Consistency can get dangerously close to rigidity, and artificially imposed uniformity is rarely practicable. Understand the limitations of both, and instead shoot for a mix of good judgment and common sense.

Negative Verbal Responses

A friend recently related a story of riding her bike past a school and hearing teachers yelling at kids from one end of the building to the other. "I'm sure glad I don't have a child at that school," she said. If you're familiar with this phenomenon, I'm sure you can appreciate what it's like for the students who have to spend so much of their lives in such an environment.

As with our attachment to punishment, there are still many adults who believe that kids won't behave or develop properly without the familiar verbal responses like scolding, criticizing, lecturing, preaching, or moralizing or that students won't take teachers seriously unless they are speaking in a loud, angry voice. In fact, these kinds of teacher behavior are so common that few question their value and appropriateness. But as one contributor noted, "Kids get numb to the sound of our voice, especially when we're intent on making them wrong. Teach the behavior you want," she said. "Don't talk it to death." Another teacher shared what she found to be a valuable piece of advice: "Say less, mean more!"

I've known teachers who recorded their interactions with students and were surprised to discover the frequency with which they were prone to communicating in negative, critical, sarcastic, or just plain *loud* ways. Pay attention to your words and your tone. When kids get a wrong answer, do you show them how to get it right or give them the correct response—without referring to their study habits, personality, or what they should have learned by now? To what degree can you resist taking a child's behavior personally? Is your feedback more long-winded than it needs to be? How often do you lose it with your students, yelling or shaming when they aren't doing what you want?

"It's not the children's emotions that teachers and staff need to manage—it's their own," wrote educator Stephen Haslam.[32] I'm not talking about the rare slip on an especially bad day. (In win-win relationships, kids will cut teachers a remarkable amount of slack for human errors.) I'm referring to patterns of verbal assaults that are rationalized with their prevalence, perpetuated by the assumption that negative feedback is necessary, and justified as an appropriate reaction to a child's behavior.[33] While there may be well-documented historical precedents for disregarding a child's dignity, these interactions can have a profoundly negative and corrosive effect on young people—the ones being attacked as well as those witnessing and hearing the interactions. Too often, the results of criticism, particularly when it attacks the character or worth of the child, tend toward a shallow, impermanent form of self-protection, with by-products like perfectionism, low confidence, and a sense of inadequacy.[34] What kids learn from shame, fear, or self-hatred is hardly what most of us want as our legacy.

"Students will always remember teachers who humiliate them, and those memories will be filled with anger and resentment," wrote Wyatt and White. "Students will also remember teachers who treated them with respect."[35] Aside from the potential for provoking even stronger or more disconnected student behaviors and attitudes, violating students' dignity and emotional safety is among the discipline strategies prohibited by the National Education Association (NEA) Code of Ethics.[36] If you want to assess the language and behaviors you use with your students, you might want to reflect on incidents by asking yourself the following questions offered by educator Bryan Cichy: "Would I have felt comfortable intervening in the same way if my colleagues had been watching? If the child's parent(s) had been watching? Did my intervention increase the child's chances of success in the long term? Would I have wanted to receive the same intervention from my superior?"[37] Anything other than an enthusiastic *yes* to all of the above will signal a need to consider other, more positive approaches to verbal interactions with your students.

Other Common Strategies (and Bad Ideas)

There are a few other patterns you're likely to observe or be encouraged to use. If you've already added any of these practices to your repertoire, please be aware of the drawbacks and limitations of each. Positive alternatives will follow.

Labeling Students

Don't put much stock in labels other teachers use to describe your students. While it may be impossible to avoid hearing that Mabel is a brain, Jackie is a slob, Monique is a pest, or Robin is pure trouble, you can refuse to allow someone else's perceptions and experiences to shape your students' chances for success in *your* room. Clear your thoughts of expectations based on gossip and give each student a fair start with a clean slate. Even positive labels are limiting and presumptuous and can impose a great deal of pressure on students. Resist the inclination to reduce a child to a simple, two-dimensional description. And using a negative, derogatory, or demeaning label to describe a student is never appropriate, whether to a colleague or a parent or to a student's face.[38]

Labeling Misbehavior

Notice how skilled some adults are at naming undesirable student behaviors, which you'll hear reflected in comments like "That's inappropriate" or "You're being disrespectful." It's hard to see the point of vague and empty criticism other than making students wrong—hardly a constructive teacher behavior. There's nothing instructive in these statements, no useful information about the desirable behaviors we'd prefer. Keep coming back to intentions to build cooperation and self-management, and use the time and energy it takes to describe a misbehavior to ask for what you want instead.

Relying on Other Adults to Deal With Student Misbehavior

This is yet another practice with plenty of history and precedents behind it. But watch out for the temptation to call parents to have them deal with a misbehaving child, or to send kids to the office or request special services, either to punish or rehabilitate misbehaving students or to get a child removed from your classroom (especially for more trivial offenses). Previous chapters have addressed more productive ways to work with administrators, support staff, and parents. Even if this is an accepted practice in your school and community, asking others to take responsibility for discipline matters reflects very poorly on you as a leader in your classroom and as a professional in general.

Expectations

You're likely to get a good bit of advice to have high expectations, and you will probably be assured that children rise to the expectations we set for them. Unfortunately, expectations, like rules, reflect the commitment of and importance to the adults who express them. They will not generate cooperation unless students also see the value in what is expected and are likewise committed—which is unlikely to happen simply because adults *expect* it of them. Don't confuse expectations with faith in kids, with a belief in their abilities, or with high-quality criteria for work assigned. There are ways to entice commitment from them. But unless they are desperate for your conditional approval (which, in itself, has some serious negative implications), simply expressing an expectation is not among them.

Failure to Follow Through

Two of the most common things teachers do to sabotage their authority reflect a lack of follow-through on previously set limits or boundaries. The first is giving warnings when a particular contingency has been breached. If you have allowed students to work together, for example, on the condition that they do so without interrupting the work anybody else is doing, yourself included, the moment they become noisy or disruptive, they lose the privilege. Warning them confirms that they don't need to respect the conditions you have set. (Pulling a series of color-coded warning cards or writing names on the board with check marks for subsequent infractions is simply an institutionalized, packaged version of the same warning process.) The second involves asking for excuses or explanations when they have misbehaved, broken an agreement, or failed to complete an assignment, for example, which suggests that they can talk their way out of the requirements you set. There are ways to build flexibility into your structures so you'll never have to use warnings or ask for excuses, and if you want to be taken seriously, avoid both of these traps.

Withholding Credit or Advancement

Of course, students need to do the work to receive credit.[39] However, allowing students' behavior to influence grading, eligibility, placement, promotion, or graduation is petty and unprofessional. These practices are also prohibited by the NEA Code of Ethics. This isn't about effort or lack of effort, or about the quality of students' work or their understanding of the concepts being taught. It's about remaining as neutral as possible in evaluating a student's work—especially on a subjective assignment like an essay, for example. If you are feeling angry at a student (or a student's parent) and think it might sway your assessment of that student's work, put it on the bottom of the pile or save it for a later time after you've had a chance to cool down. The same thing goes if you're in a generally negative space about other things going on in your life. Wait until you're in a place where you can see and appreciate the positive evidence of their efforts.

Telling Students How Their Behavior Makes You Feel

This is another popular strategy that just won't go away, so don't be surprised to hear people recommend statements like "When you forget your assignment, I feel frustrated and disappointed" or "I get angry when it's so noisy in here" to keep your kids in line. Your students are not responsible for your emotional well-being, and you really do not want to put them in that position, if only for the possibility that they simply may not care enough for this approach to work. (Wouldn't you prefer that students return library books so they can get a new one rather than having them do so to avoid your anger and disappointment or to gain your conditional approval?) People rationalize using these statements as a means of teaching empathy, but the responses I have witnessed tend more toward stress, resentment, or indifference instead. Caretaking has its costs, so even if this does seem to work, it's a strategy you really want to avoid. There are ways to build empathy and compassion for others—as well as ways to motivate cooperation and respect—without burdening anyone with the job of keeping you happy.[40]

Praise

You'll probably hear that praise is the go-to strategy for motivating and reinforcing positive behavior, but there are a slew of problems here as well. First of all, praising kids to *motivate* them is a misuse of a reinforcer, which only works *after* a behavior has appeared.[41] Second, praise is misused again when it attempts to distract a child from a problem, discount a problem a child is having, or make a child feel better. Finally, even used as a reinforcer after the fact, praise tends to reflect a personal judgment, approval contingent on certain behavioral choices students have made. Spontaneous, random, and genuine expressions of affection and appreciation are fine—assuming there's no agenda or conditionality attached. But if you want to build responsibility and reinforce positive choices, go for the more neutral acknowledgment in a recognition statement that does not rely on your reaction. (See the next chapter, "Create a Win-Win Classroom.")

Projection

If you've ever heard someone tell a child "You must be proud" or "You should be thankful," you've witnessed examples of adults projecting their feelings and values onto the child. This strategy is usually fairly innocuous, and more presumptuous than dangerous, although I've seen it used to deliberately attempt to reinforce something the teacher wanted the child to continue doing. The problem is that something like "You must be happy" presumes students feel a certain way, although the experience may hold an entirely different meaning or value to them. As an alternative, you can share your observations ("You're obviously excited about this" or "You seem pleased"), ask students how they feel, or simply recognize the accomplishment ("You worked very hard on this!").[42]

Tokens

This idea has also been around for a long time, referring to a reinforcement system that uses some tangible reward—a sticker, ticket, chip, gold star, piece of candy, or other items to which a student attaches value—to acknowledge the performance of a desired behavior. Even in the 1970s, research revealed that this strategy was often overused and was discouraged as not necessarily the most effective reinforcement strategy in the long run.[43] However, those of us desperate enough to try it soon discovered that it was hard to avoid being arbitrary in how we ended up distributing the tokens, that the system was unwieldy and time-consuming, and that after a while, the classic "token inflation" would indeed rear its ugly head—in my case, when kids started asking whether they were getting tickets for going to lunch. While I know teachers who indulge their students' enjoyment of stickers (especially the scratch-and-sniff variety, and yes, this includes high school kids), the ones who do it successfully tend to do it infrequently and uniformly, say, for every student who turns in a particular assignment or project. Nonetheless, look to desirable activities and privileges kids can earn for more motivational leverage.

Physical Punishment

It's pretty sad that we still need to address this topic at this point in our history and social evolution, but as of late summer 2009, there were still twenty states in the United States that permit children to be paddled in school.[44] I'd like to think that it goes without saying that there is no place for physical punishment in a win-win classroom, regardless of the apparent justification. Although often touted as a last resort, there is far too much evidence of the practice invoked as a first response, often to trivial infractions. Research speaks to a wide range of negative outcomes of corporal punishment—not just for the children being hit but for their classmates and the climate of the school, too—including a tendency to make behavior even worse. Again, think in terms of the honorable intentions schools profess and consider the insanity, much less hypocrisy, of using physical punishment to teach things like respect, self-control, or nonviolence. Hitting children makes us look weak, ineffective, unskilled, and unprofessional. Even if your school condones this practice, don't. If you cannot teach without hitting children, you do not have the skills you need to be allowed in the classroom with them. There are better ways.[45]

Attitudinal Obstacles

OK, so these aren't strategies as much as stumbling blocks. Attitudinal obstacles tend to show up in a couple different ways. One is a resistance to having to motivate kids in the first place. I still hear people insist that students should want to learn for the love of learning and that the satisfaction gained from new knowledge and personal growth should be motivation and reinforcement enough. While few people would argue with the desire for such evidence of self-actualization, you may have to stretch a bit to entice some of your students, especially those who have yet to experience the joys of successfully exploring a school subject they just loved.

There is no such thing as unmotivated behavior—for kids or for adults—and few people are willing to put in time and effort if nothing good comes of it, whether the outcome or payoff is pleasure, satisfaction, achievement, a grade, or a paycheck. (I haven't met many teachers who profess an eagerness to teach exclusively for the love of teaching. And few kids are likely to get excited about work they perceive as boring, irrelevant, or impossible to do.) Clearly, some outcomes are more effective than others, and in case you're worried about the idea that you're bribing a student any time you offer a positive outcome, keep in mind that the threat of punishment or a teacher's angry tirade is just as much a bribe as a chance to work on an enrichment activity, move on to the next book, or work with a partner.

The second obstacle is evident in the mindset that resists the need to differentiate how we motivate or reinforce different students. It's easy to fall back on old standbys like "If I let one do it, I have to let them all do it," but the truth is there will always be students who couldn't care less about whatever *it* is and would just as soon have a chance to work on an art project, work at a computer, or do their assignments sitting on the floor as, say, run an errand, work in a group, or have the rest of the period off to visit the media center or start in on their homework. Different kids, different strategies, and it's the creative and attentive teachers who best connect what they want to what their individual students want.

Finally, there is the obstacle that comes up any time you block an idea or talk yourself out of doing something you think might work with your kids for fear of repercussions. Absolutely proceed with caution when it comes to a strategy or accommodation that's never been tried successfully in your school, or when you approach an administrator or department chair for something that is generally discouraged in your setting. But know that just because it may seem easier to assume "we can't do that" than it is to make a case for what you want to do, in many cases, you can pull off more than you think you can. Many of the strategies involved in becoming a win-win teacher are, as you can see, somewhat outside the traditions practiced in some settings. If you have people rushing to support you in these endeavors—and some teachers do—all the better. But if you find yourself feeling boxed in by restrictions and obstacles, start small and do what you need to do to avoid drawing fire to yourself. Many of these ideas (for example, how you talk to students or your willingness to connect with them) have no impact on others and will happen, for the most part, behind closed doors with little risk of putting your job on the line. Resist the status quo, especially when it includes practices that hurt kids and make things more difficult for you, and don't let yourself be paralyzed by other people's limited thinking. Question tradition, and if you choose a particular strategy or approach, do it consciously, not just because that's what everybody else is doing or because that's the way it's always been done. Your ideas won't always work the way you want or get the support you'd like, but within the walls of your classroom and the relationships you create with your students, keep looking for the most win-win options possible. (See the next chapter, "Create a Win-Win Classroom," for additional positive alternatives.)

ACTIVITY

1. Which of the ineffective classroom-management strategies mentioned in this chapter were familiar to you from your training?

2. Which of the strategies have you observed in your school?

3. Which of the strategies have you tried yourself?

4. Which do you think will be the hardest to avoid or stop using? (Read the next chapter, "Create a Win-Win Classroom," for some additional effective alternatives.)

NOTES

1. Quoted in Quimby (2003, para. 3).

2. Reynolds and Reynolds (2008, para. 1).

3. Quoted in Naylor (2009).

4. This child's brief school history included several learning problems and a fairly extensive behavioral pathology, including some disturbing self-harming behaviors. I have met very few individuals who presented this range and intensity of dysfunction at this age, and few who benefited more from making a connection with a safe adult in the classroom, a process that ended up being more remedial than any cognitive or punitive intervention attempted. Thank you to my friend and former editor Matthew Diener for jogging my memory and for the suggestion to kick this chapter off with this story.

5. Marshall (n.d.).

6. "School Violence: The History of School Discipline" (1998, para. 1).

7. Education professor Jonathan Zimmerman (2007) wrote that strict discipline has been under fire since "the very birth of the common school system in the 1830s" and that objections have come "from a host of different Americans. The most prominent champion of common schools, Horace Mann, warned teachers against excessive force and the suppression of students' natural inclinations. To reformers like John Dewey, schools based on strict discipline—and its pedagogical companion, rote memorization—could never give citizens the skills they needed to govern themselves. Instead of fostering mindless obedience, then, schools needed to teach children how to make up their own minds—that is, how to reason, deliberate and rule on complex political questions" (para. 7).

8. Purkey and Aspy (1988, p. 47).

9. To explore these issues in greater detail, please check out *The Win-Win Classroom* (Bluestein, 2008) and *Creating Emotionally Safe Schools* (Bluestein, 2001).

10. Gazzaniga (1988, p. 205). The sense of power or the ability to impact situations affecting your life also has implications for your body and physical health. In an article on the impact of stress on coronary health, Anne Underwood (2005) reported, "People respond differently to high-pressure work situation. The key to whether it produces a coronary seems to be whether you have a sense of control over life, or live at the mercy of circumstances and superiors" (p. 51).

11. Gatto (2005, p. 6).

12. "NYCLU, Annenberg Institute Release Report on Successful and Safe NYC Schools That Say No to Aggressive Police Tactics" (2009). This report studied the impact of aggressive controlling approaches in schools with high-risk populations. The studies affirmed that "there are effective, real-world alternatives to making schools feel like jails" (para. 4) and, quoting Tara Bahl, data and research analyst for the Annenberg Institute for School Reform, determined that "the successful schools' policies and practices emphasize the students' dignity, their desire to learn, and their capacity for responsible decision making. They have created a culture where positive educational outcomes are common and expected and they've put students on the path toward graduation" (para. 10). The report concluded, "These punitive measures contribute to the school to prison pipeline, a system of local, state and federal education and public safety policies that pushes students out of school and into the criminal justice system. The pipeline disproportionately affects youth of color and youth with disabilities" (para. 15).

13. Isaacson (2007, p. 26).

14. From the BrainyQuote website: http://www.brainyquote.com/quotes/authors/r/ralph_nader.html.

15. Liability issues are almost never mentioned, though if we're going to be honest here, they probably drive the need for things like discipline codes and posting rules (with or without the negative consequences) throughout the school or in student handbooks as much as any other concern expressed.

16. Mann (n.d., para. 9).

17. Marshall (2001, p. 49).

18. Please do not hear this as an argument for denying kids a chance to at least do their homework in detention. I've never known detention to work as a discipline strategy and will always vote for more sensible ways to shape kids' behavior, but this is at least a decent use of the time.

19. Marshall (2001, p. 49).

20. With regard to detention, Marvin Marshall (2001) noted, "Students who are assigned to detention and fail to serve it are punished with more detention. . . . In the hundreds of seminars I have conducted around the world, teachers who use detention rarely suggest that it is effective in changing behavior. If detention were effective, the same students would not be consistently assigned to it" (p. 48). To support Marshall's comments, a teacher in one of my seminars sent me a copy of her district's tardiness policy. The "consequences for excessive tardies" included escalating punishments: one afternoon of detention for the first through fourth unexcused tardy, two detentions for the fifth through eighth incident, three for nine to twelve tardies, and four for thirteen through sixteen late arrivals to class. The list concluded with the following warning: "Failure to stay for afterschool detention will result in out-of-school suspension." If this policy is the only incentive for kids to get to class on time, clearly something isn't working. In addition, I'm trying to imagine the record keeping for policies like these, and really have to wonder what this district is trying to accomplish.

21. Freiberg (2007c).

22. Blum et al. (2002, p. 12).

23. Kenmore (n.d., para. 2).

24. Littke and Grabelle (2004, p. 44).

25. Bluestein and Katz (2005, p. 15).

26. Mahoney and Purr (2007, pp. 24, 36). Instead, they suggested, "spend the time doing something to get to know their names and personalities" and allow "limited, structured time to catch up with each other."

27. If you think about it, this single rule is actually quite restrictive, and even preschool kids can get their heads around its meaning. You will want to have specific instructions on how to use certain equipment, or which behaviors will allow kids to continue working on a specific task, but the simpler your rules and limits, the more effective they tend to be.

28. Note that most people generally want the school to do more than manage children's behavior. An editorial requesting that schools stress moral learning in place of listing rules quoted one adult as saying, "Am I the only parent who wants her children to learn to reason rather than memorize a set of behavioral rules?" (Blumenfeld, 1996).

29. Teachers tend to favor students who are more affluent or dress well, as well as kids with superior athletic or academic skills. Likewise, research indicates that minority students are more likely to receive harsher and more frequent penalties for the same misbehaviors observed in nonminority students. Bluestein (2001).

30. Adler and Springen (1999).

31. Teachers report the greatest opposition from colleagues and administrators when they attempt to meet individual learning needs with neurologically appropriate accommodations,

especially if they are working with administrators who insist that students uniformly sit quietly and still. They also report greater success with the support of counselors, occupational therapists, and often parents. Likewise, some have made strides by starting with small and nondisruptive interventions, and by demonstrating (and documenting) the positive impact of these accommodations with improved student behavior and academic performance.

32. Haslam (2001).

33. This type of teacher behavior is often a sign of burnout or extreme stress and may not even be related to the kids themselves. When you find yourself taking things out on your students or feeling contempt for them or the job, please consider asking for help to sort out whatever is going on in your life or to develop better coping mechanisms. (See the next section, "Part IV: Self," for more on self-care.)

34. How often have you met high-achieving individuals who are terrified of making a mistake and see only flaws in their finest accomplishments? How many adults do you know who believe they're "no good at drawing (or math or writing, for example)," or who lack faith in their appearance or social skills because of some reckless comment addressed to them years earlier?

35. Wyatt and White (2007, pp. 53–54).

36. These behaviors include attempts to threaten emotional safety by humiliating, expressing contempt, condemning or attacking students' behavior or attitude, condemning or attacking their values, violating dignity or self-worth, criticizing, shaming, engaging in verbal or emotional violence, yelling, intimidating, threatening, using sarcasm, controlling, manipulating, punishing, employing conditional approval or love, or using the threat of emotional abandonment. National Education Association (1975).

37. Cichy (2008).

38. Note the difference between describing a behavior ("You worked hard on this" or "Your handwriting has really improved") and describing a student ("You're so smart, or neat, or good"). Likewise, rather than labeling needy kids as pests, give them a time you'll be available or assign them to a partner. If they get the answers wrong, explaining the skill again or in a different way will teach them the skill far more effectively than impatience, criticism, or any label that suggests that they are lacking in intelligence or worth.

39. Hopefully, you will be assigning work that they can do successfully so that they perceive this to be possible.

40. Students motivated by the need to please, gain approval, or avoid someone's reactions often have a really hard time making decisions in their own best interests. For more information on this topic, there is a free article on my website (www.janebluestein.com/articles/whatswrong .html): "What's Wrong with 'I-Messages.'"

41. This is more common in primary classrooms, where you'll often hear things like "I like the way Susie is sitting" to try to get others in the class to sit quietly. As an alternative, try tying your request to an outcome that does not depend on your students' need for your conditional approval, that is, for you to like them, too. Be aware that even young kids can tell when you're just saying something nice to get them to do what you want.

42. Adapted from Bluestein (2008).

43. Osborn and Osborn (1977, p. 38).

44. Thanks to Jordan Riak and Parents and Teachers Against Violence in Education (http://nospank.net).

45. For more research and information on this topic, there is an excerpt from *Creating Emotionally Safe Schools* (Bluestein, 2001), "Spare the Rod," on my website (www.janebluestein .com/articles/no_paddling.html).

Chapter 9

Understand the Behaviors of Students With Emotional and/or Behavioral Disorders

Roger Pierangelo and George Giuliani

Understanding Challenging Behaviors

Great strides have been taken in the education of children with disabilities since the enactment of P.L. 94-142, the Education of the Handicapped Act (EHA). However, areas of concern remain. The federal definition refers to special education as "specially designed instruction, at no cost to parents, to meet the *unique needs of a child* [emphasis added] with a disability" (34 CFR 300.17[a]). Too often, however, when working with students with challenging behaviors, methodology has focused more on controlling behavior than on addressing the *needs* underlying the behavior and instruction toward more appropriate ways of getting those needs met.

Challenging Behaviors Serve a Function for the Student

Challenging behaviors (or sets or chains of behaviors) are always directed at achieving a desired outcome. In essence, such behaviors exist because they serve a useful purpose for the student. The behavior has worked in some way to meet a need for the student in the past, and the student will continue to use it because it has worked.

Although challenging behaviors may be socially inappropriate, from the student's perspective, they are reasonable and logical responses to events that have occurred in their environment (e.g., responses to a reprimand, teacher direction, or a bad headache).

Many students with significant skill deficits use challenging behaviors because they have no other means for successfully influencing their environment or communicating their needs. Challenging behaviors may be viewed as basic forms of communication (e.g., crying to indicate hunger) or social interaction (e.g., clowning around to initiate social interactions). Other, more socially skilled students use challenging behaviors because they are the most efficient or effective way to achieve a desired outcome.

Functions of behavior can be divided roughly according to two purposes: "to get something" or "to avoid or escape something." When a student's behavior functions to get something, it means that the student's teacher or peers respond to a challenging behavior by giving the student attention, approval, or tangibles. For example, name-calling may result in giggles from peers, acting out may result in a trip to the gym to "cool off," or scribbling on class work may result in extra teacher assistance on a worksheet.

When a student's challenging behavior functions to avoid or escape something, it means that the teacher or peers respond to a challenging behavior by stopping an event that the student finds unpleasant. For example, whining and complaining after each direction may result in a teacher's lessening demands, or threatening to hit a peer may result in the cessation of teasing.

It is important to note that the form of behavior (how a student acts) is not necessarily related to function. For example, a student may say, "Leave me alone," in an effort to bring greater teacher attention (e.g., the teacher responds by saying, "Come on. You don't really mean that. Let's do . . ."). It is impossible to identify function accurately just by describing student actions. Function can only be determined by describing student's interactions within the environment.

Challenging Behaviors Are Context Related

A behavior occurs because of what precedes or follows it. Challenging behaviors do not occur in a vacuum but rather because certain environmental or ecological variables have induced them to occur. These variables can be identified through careful analysis and assessment.

Several general classes of context variables influence behaviors. One such class is *immediate antecedents,* referring to events that occur just prior to the challenging behavior. Such events trigger an immediate reaction from the student. Examples of immediate antecedents include a teacher direction, a difficult work task, a reprimand, or peer teasing.

Setting events is a second general class and refers to context variables that occur concurrently with the behavior of concern or at an earlier time. Setting events work to "set the stage" for a challenging behavior to occur. They include setting characteristics such as seating arrangements or the schedule of classroom activities; prior social interactions such as a fight on the bus on the way to school; and physical conditions of the student such as illness, fatigue, or allergies.

Another, broader class of context variables that influence behaviors is *lifestyle factors.* Although often difficult to identify precisely, such factors contribute to the overall quality of one's life. The presence or absence of such factors as participation in personally meaningful activities, the opportunity for choice and control, inclusion in typical school and community activities, friendships, and good relationships with family members and others can have a profound influence on the behaviors that students exhibit day to day. Because positive life experiences provide the motivation for learning, they are necessary conditions for the success of behavioral support and interventions.

Effective Interventions Are Based on a Thorough Understanding of the Challenging Behavior

Effective interventions result in long-term behavioral change. To produce long-term results, effective interventions must directly address the function and contextual influences of the challenging behavior. Once challenging behaviors are understood in terms of the outcomes they produce for a student, the goal is to replace challenging behaviors with socially acceptable alternatives that will help the student to achieve the same outcomes. If challenging behaviors reflect a skill deficit, then the solution is to teach acceptable alternatives. Interventions that ignore function by simply trying to suppress (e.g., punish) a behavior are likely to fail because the student's needs remain unmet. Even students who know how to behave appropriately, but do not, can benefit from instruction. Students can learn that appropriate behaviors are effective and efficient means for achieving desired results.

For Example:

- *A student stops working and starts talking to classmates.* The teacher might assume that the student is being noncompliant. If the teacher can recognize that the student is anxious because the lesson is not understood, the teacher can teach the student to recognize and express the need for help and to ask for and obtain assistance.
- *A student puts his head down on his or her desk.* The teacher might assume that the student is being disrespectful. However, if the teacher knows that the student typically puts his head down when he has a headache, the teacher might ask him if his head hurts, teach him to express his need, and allow him either to see the school nurse or to leave his head down until he feels better (Topper, Williams, Leo, Hamilton, & Fox, 1994).

Effective interventions also address the contextual influences of behavior. Once the contextual influences of a challenging behavior are understood, the goal is to prevent that behavior from occurring by changing the environment. Prevention strategies can be as simple as modifying an assignment or changing the pace of instruction to avoid student frustration, or they can be as complex as modifying morning routines at home or learning experiences at school to match student needs. Interventions that focus on changing the student's behavior without also addressing the behavior's contextual influences are likely to fail because the student's situation (the one that produces the challenging behavior) remains unchanged.

Understand the Difference Between Symptoms and Problems

One of the most important concepts to know when working with children with emotional disturbances is the difference between a symptom and a problem. Understanding this difference will be crucial when it comes time to develop a treatment plan or a functional behavioral assessment. Many times, teachers will mistake a symptom for a problem and miss the opportunity to identify the real issues in a more timely manner.

As emotional problems (e.g., conflicts, fears, insecurities, vulnerabilities) develop, the pressure from these issues forms tension. This tension can only be released in one of two ways: verbally or behaviorally. If the children are unable to label their feelings correctly, then the tension will vent in behavior, or what we call behavioral symptoms. That is why counseling or therapy can be beneficial to a child, because part of the process involves identifying and labeling conflicts so that the child can talk out the tension.

Usually, the more serious the problem(s), the greater the level of tension. A high level of tension will need to be released through several symptomatic behaviors. Therefore, the more serious the problem(s), the greater frequency, intensity, and duration of the behavioral symptoms. Further, high levels of tension result in more immediate behavioral symptoms. As a result, the behaviors may be inappropriate and impulsive rather than well thought out.

As the child becomes more confident or learns to work out problems (e.g, through therapy, classroom management, intervention strategies, etc.), the underlying problems become smaller. What results is a decrease in the levels of tension and consequently lower frequency, intensity, and duration of the inappropriate, impulsive, or self-destructive behavior patterns.

Normally, these behavioral symptoms are the first signal noticed by teachers, parents, and professionals. If this pattern is not fully understood, both the child and the teacher will become very frustrated during attempts to extinguish the symptoms. Identifying symptoms as indicators of something more serious is another first step in helping children work out their problems.

Behaviors That May Be Indicative of More Serious Problems

Examples of typical symptomatic behavior patterns that may be indicative of more serious problems may include the following:

- Anxiety
- Constantly blames others for problems
- Controlling
- Defies authority
- Distractible
- Fearful of adults
- Fearful of new situations
- Fears criticism
- Gives many excuses for inappropriate behavior
- Hyperactive
- Impulsivity

- Inflexibility
- Intrusive
- Irresponsibility
- Moody
- Overly critical
- Overreactive
- Panics easily
- Physical with others
- Poor judgment
- Procrastinates
- Rarely takes chances
- Short attention span
- Tires easily
- Unable to focus on task
- Verbally hesitant

Once these behaviors are noticed, the teacher should evaluate the seriousness of the situation by applying three rules (Pierangelo, 2004).

1. *What is the frequency of the symptoms?* Consider how often the symptoms occur. The more serious the problem, the greater amount of tension generated. The greater the amount of tension, the more frequent will be the need to release it. Therefore, the greater the frequency of the symptom, the greater chance that the problem(s) are serious and should be handled immediately with the help of the special education teacher or psychologist.

2. *What is the duration of the symptoms?* The more serious the problem, the greater the degree of tension generated. The greater the degree of tension, the longer the student will need to release it. Therefore, the longer the duration of the symptoms, the more serious the problem.

3. *What is the intensity of the symptoms?* The more serious the problem, the more intense the level of resulting tension will be. This level of tension will require a more intense release.

Symptomatic Behaviors Exhibited When a Child Has Low Levels of Tension

When students possess low levels of tension, they exhibit what are called positive behavior symptoms more often than not. In school, for instance, the child will exhibit (more often than not) behaviors that include the following:

- Adequate organizational skills
- Age-appropriate attention span
- Appropriate memory
- Consistency
- Flexibility
- Good concentration
- Responsibility with school work

Parents will see positive behavior symptoms resulting from low levels of tension such as the following:

- Appropriate judgment
- No problems falling asleep
- Normal strivings for parental approval
- Resiliency
- Willingness to reason
- Willingness to try

Again, keep in mind that these patterns may vary to some degree during adolescence and still be within normal limits.

Socially, children with low tension levels will (more often than not) be able to

- maintain social interactions;
- show willingness to try new social experiences; and
- treat peers appropriately.

Symptomatic Behaviors Exhibited When a Child Has High Levels of Tension

However, according to Pierangelo and Giuliani (2006), when serious conflicts arise, the available energy must be drained away to deal with the conflicts like white blood cells to an infection. Because energy must be drained away, less energy is available to keep things in perspective and maintain consistency. When you observe a pattern of behavior that is inappropriate and results in serious symptoms, you should automatically become aware that some serious problem may exist.

When a child has high levels of tension, negative behavior patterns will be exhibited. When this occurs, the negative patterns may show up at school in the following ways:

- Disorganization
- Inability to focus on task
- Inflexibility
- Irresponsibility
- Procrastination
- Projecting the reasons for problems on everyone and everything else

A parent may observe negative behavior patterns at home such as the following:

- Forgetfulness
- Overreactions
- Oversensitivity
- Unwillingness to reason
- Unwillingness to venture out

When high levels of tension exist, they may interfere in social functioning. For example, one may observe the student

- withdrawing from social situations;
- constantly finding fault with peers;
- being unwilling to try new social experiences; or
- express social fears or beliefs that no one likes him or her.

If therapy is required, be aware that it can be a long-term process, especially if the problems have been around for a long time. Consequently, the treatment approach may need to combine outside therapy, family therapy, and classroom behavior management. After these interventions have taken place, you can tell if your student is making progress by the reduction of the frequency, intensity, and duration of the negative symptomatic behavior patterns. Also, be aware that some parents may resist therapy, leaving your classroom management techniques as the only intervention strategy. These will be discussed in further chapters.

Redirecting Students to More Appropriate Behaviors

Many approaches may be effective in redirecting students to more appropriate behaviors when a challenging situation appears to be developing. The goal for educators is to help the student decrease emotional intensity while conveying that they are there to support the student and to understand why the student is having a hard time. Adults who are successful at supporting a student through a difficult time are seen by the student as unconditionally caring, trustworthy, able to protect them from harm and humiliation, confident that the student can cope with excessive stress, and confident that the future will be better.

The following techniques and strategies are offered as options for redirecting students to more appropriate behaviors. *It is important to tailor interventions to the developmental level of the student.* These options are not intended to be the sole interventions to increase a positive behavior; rather, they are examples of how inappropriate behaviors may be de-escalated or redirected so as to avoid the need for more intrusive interventions.

As with all interventions, teams will want to choose techniques and strategies that support the return of the student to appropriate behaviors rather than approaches that inadvertently reinforce negative behaviors.

Interest Boosting

When students' behavior indicates that they are drifting away from attending to the task or activity, some additional information related to their interests or experiences is helpful to pique their attention or interest in the activity. For example, when leading a discussion about music, the staff member might ask the students about their personal stereo equipment to boost their interest in the discussion.

Planned Ignoring

This technique is more successful if planned before the behavior occurs. It is most effective when a student is trying to get attention or to provoke staff members, as long as other students are not involved. Not calling on the student to run an errand or ignoring the student while telling several other students what a good job they are doing are examples of this technique. It is important to provide a positive reinforcer as soon as an appropriate behavior is exhibited; be ready to reinforce the correct behavior the moment it appears. Do not use this technique for severe behavior problems. "Remember that there is a qualitative difference between ignoring a person's behavior and ignoring a person. Find a way to minimize attention given to a behavior and continue to offer support" (Topper et al., 1994).

Providing More Information

Clarifying expectations and experiences in a form compatible with the person's assessed learning style helps to ensure that the student is not reacting to some misunderstanding or misperception of the activity or interaction (see Boeckmann, Cardelli, and Jacobs, 1989).

Tension Reduction Through Humor

Frequently, a problem or potential problem may be defused with a joke or a lighthearted comment. Many times, anxiety, fear, or a challenge will make the student feel obligated or forced to react negatively. Humor can act as a pressure release valve to allow the student to laugh off something without a negative response—to "save face," in other words. This technique may be effective when the student has responded instinctively in a negative fashion or appears to be wanting to retaliate but is indecisive concerning whether or how to do so. Never use satire or ridicule and be aware if student "reads" an attempt at humor as ridicule; the student must correctly read the caring aspect of the interaction.

Acknowledging the Message

Acknowledging, in a nonjudgmental fashion, the message or emotion expressed through a challenging behavior, even when we are unable to honor the message or condone its form, can serve as a prelude to other strategies and help set the stage for a successful and respectful outcome (e.g., "I know it is hard to wait your turn . . ."). Acknowledgment may also help to teach the "right words to say" by positively restating the person's behaviorally expressed message (Boeckmann et al., 1989).

Signal Interference

This technique includes signaling the student with nonverbal indications when behavior is beginning to be inappropriate (e.g., snapping fingers, holding up hand to indicate "stop"). This is most useful for behaviors that are mild in nature when they have just begun to escalate.

Proximity Control

When a student's behavior is beginning to be disruptive or distracting, the staff member moves close to the student while carrying on the activity with the whole group. No punishment or undue attention is given to the student at the time. Generally, the adult's presence at close range is enough to subdue mild inappropriate behaviors. Be attentive to whether the student may perceive proximity as a threat.

Hurdle Help

A staff member provides immediate instruction at the very moment the student experiences trouble to help him or her over the hurdle of dealing appropriately with others. A timely comment at the onset of the problem may help the student follow the correct course of action. For example, when a staff member sees a student bunching up a piece of paper and preparing to throw it, the staff member reminds the student to walk to the trash can to throw it away. Timing is essential with this strategy.

Restructuring Routine

While routine has a stabilizing effect on everyone, sometimes students tire of it. Adjusting to energy level provides the opportunity for a student to be refreshed. Shifts in routine should be occasional so as not to disrupt the orderliness of a planned, sequenced routine (e.g., rescheduling TV time to allow students to watch a special program after the group has completed tasks). Note that students with severe behavior problems may require visual reminders of routines, such as personal schedules of their activities on their desks. Changes should be explained and integrated into any visual tracking system the student is using.

Making a Direct Appeal to Values

Students are encouraged to make a decision as to whether their behavior is helping the situation. One-on-one conferencing may elicit an understanding of how the behavior may be making matters worse and to discover alternate behaviors that can help the students focus on the matter at hand and their part in it. A questioning format is most effective here, beginning with questions that require a yes answer (to develop a positive attitude) and phasing in questions that require a more involved answer (e.g., Where did this happen? What did you do then? How do you feel about that? Why do you think you responded in this way?). Finally, seek out some sort of commitment for continuing a behavior or stopping a behavior next time the problem occurs.

Distraction

When a confrontation or a negative behavior is creating a disturbance, focusing the group's attention and/or the individual's attention on something different can reduce or eliminate the problem. A student who is screaming may stop to listen if the staff member begins discussing a topic of interest to the student or if the staff member begins an activity with the other students that the student would enjoy. This technique helps the student to give up the negative behavior by providing an opportunity to make the choice to do so and prevents the staff member from having to use more restrictive interventions.

Infusion With Affection

Often a very positive, supportive, and appreciative approach may help a student to respond more appropriately. A warm, open, caring response from a staff member may help the student talk about the problems being experienced before the problems build into a significant incident. An example might be, "I think you probably feel very sad now, and that makes me feel bad, too. Do you think we might walk and be able to talk about what happened?"

Regrouping

When a student is having trouble within a group, it is often helpful to move the student to another group or space to avoid continuing problems. This is not a punishing "kick-out" but an attempt to offer the student an environment that will help the child maintain control of the behavior. For example, "I think this new location will be better for you and allow you to be in control of yourself. I can see you're trying."

The Antiseptic Bounce

When a student's behavior indicates a build-up of stress or restlessness, it may be helpful to remove the student in such a way that attention is not focused on the negative behavior. For example, a pass to the office to run an errand may be enough to defuse a potential problem and allow the student to return fresh to the activity. This allows a few minutes away from the problem area without confrontation about behavior and may provide enough of a release and a distraction to enable the student to return to the program in a new frame of mind.

Limiting Supplies and Materials

When a student begins to misuse, abuse, or otherwise cause a problem with tools or supplies, it may be advisable to limit continuing access to the material at that time. This requires a calm voice and a supportive stance if de-escalation is desired.

Interpretation As Interference

A student may not understand or be aware of a behavior that is occurring. Sometimes it may be helpful to describe to students what they are doing by commenting on observable behavior. This technique serves as a reminder that the behavior is inappropriate. For example, "When you talk while I am talking, not only is it hard for you to listen, but it is hard for others to listen, too."

Being a Role Model

The most significant management tool available to staff members is conducting themselves in the manner in which students are expected to behave. Staff members who demonstrate self-control, respect for others, good manners, courtesy, honesty, fairness, and good judgment teach by example. Students with serious behavior issues often attend to the emotional tone of the speaker with more concentration than they give to the actual words. Clear, calm words may be modeled by other students and immediately diffuse a tense situation. For example, "Mrs. Walsh says it's not my job to worry about Johnny. My job is _____ right now."

Pacing Indicator

Some students, especially those with severe disabilities, lose the ability of language when protesting an activity choice. Shifting the student to "break time" and asking the student to rejoin the instructional activity when ready can be effective in diffusing escalating behaviors. For example, giving a student an object that signifies break time (e.g., a magazine, small stuffed animal, a felt heart), to be returned when the student is ready, may de-escalate behavior and provide for choice making.

More Tips on Neutralizing
or Momentarily Calming the Immediate Situation

1. Think about what message you are communicating by
   - your position and proximity to the student (e.g., avoid being a threat, avoid chasing, avoid getting hurt, keep the student safe);
   - how quickly or slowly you are talking or moving;

- your tone of voice;
- the intensity of your response (e.g., if the student is loud, then you need to be calm and quiet).

2. Try not to focus on the struggle; think about what you want the student to do instead (i.e., ideally what the situation should look like).

3. Take into consideration that the student may be scared, confused, and embarrassed and may need to "save face." Provide a fair and logical option to calm the moment.

4. Whenever possible, continue the flow of the day. This will minimize focusing on the "problem behavior."

5. When safety is an issue, interrupt the behavior to avoid injury but do so by supporting, not punishing, the person.

6. Remember there is a qualitative difference between ignoring a person's behavior and ignoring a person.

7. If necessary, adjust the environment to keep things from getting worse.

8. If you think your response is making things worse, stop and re-evaluate.

9. Others should continue with their regular day—if you need help, tell others what they should do. If another teacher is dealing with a difficult situation, refrain from intervening unless asked to do so (Topper et al., 1994).

Ways to Maintain Positive Changes in Student Behavior

The success of any plan to change student behaviors depends on the willingness and ability of the student to continue to use the appropriate behavior without excessive outside support (i.e., the intervention). The most basic way to ensure maintenance of behavior change is to be sure that interventions teach the student a set of skills. Teaching skills requires IEP teams to include strategies in the behavioral intervention plan to teach the student in such a way as to promote the maintenance (i.e., lasting over time, even when the extrinsic reinforcers have faded) and generalization (i.e., using the behavior in other appropriate settings) of replacement behaviors. One strategy for doing this is to restructure the social environment to leverage the power of peer relationships to promote positive behavior. These behaviors are then maintained though the natural consequences of having and being with friends. Indeed, in numerous instances, students have been taught to encourage or reinforce appropriate behavior and to ignore or walk away from negative provocations of their classmates.

Another way to promote long-lasting behavior change is to use strategies based on cognitive mediation (i.e., thinking through a situation before acting on emotion) and self-management (i.e., using techniques to control one's own behavior). For example, students have been taught to apply various problem-solving strategies by engaging in positive self-talk (e.g., telling themselves, "I know how to get out of this argument without having to use my fists,") or self-cueing (e.g., recognizing that their jaws are clenched, they are getting upset, and they need to ask to be excused). Students also are taught to do the following:

- *Self-monitor.* Count the frequency or duration of their own behavior.
- *Self-evaluate.* Compare the change in their behavior to a certain standard to determine whether they are making progress or not.
- *Self-reinforce.* Give themselves rewards when their behavior has reached certain criteria.

For example, Gloria may be taught to count and record the number of times she appropriately raises her hand and waits to be called on during class discussion. She can then determine whether she has met the daily criteria of at least three hand-raises. She then can look at her record of hand-raises for the week, determine if she is making progress toward her goal or not, and collect points to use at the class store later in the week.

Some interventions should be implemented indefinitely, while others will eventually need to stop. For example, Julio is learning to use social problem-solving skills instead of getting into fights on the playground (an intervention that we hope Julio will use forever). He is learning to ask for adult support when he feels like he might get into a fight, and his team has decided that he can earn points for the class token economy when he seeks help appropriately rather than fighting (an intervention that must end at some point). Knowing that he cannot get points for the rest of his life, the team has decided to use the technique of fading once Julio has reached a certain criterion; that is, Julio's teachers will gradually decrease the use of points or other tangible rewards.

This could be done in several ways. First, his teacher could increase the amount of time Julio has to remain "fight-free" to receive a reward. For example, he may initially receive rewards daily, but as he reaches criterion, the time between rewards could be increased to every other day, then once a week, and so on. Another way to fade the intervention is for his teacher to award him fewer points until he is receiving no points at all. For instance, Julio could initially earn 50 points per day for not fighting. This could be reduced to 40, then 30, and so on. It is very important to note that the social reinforcement should continue and eventually replace the tangible rewards. If this process is gradual and Julio is helped to realize the advantages of using appropriate social problem solving, remaining fight-free will become intrinsically rewarding to him.

The success of these strategies may depend on providing the student with periodic "booster" training to review the instruction used in the original intervention plan. Some students also may need to receive self-advocacy training to teach them how to ask for positive recognition or call attention to positive changes in their behavior appropriately. This is especially important for students who have such bad reputations that adults and peers do not recognize when their behaviors are changing. Finally, school personnel can support changes in student performance by accepting "barely noticeable differences," incremental changes that reflect the fact the student is taking positive steps toward the desired goal.

Whole-Classroom Instructional Strategies

Following are suggestions for several programming elements that facilitate positive behavior. This material is not intended to be exhaustive; rather, elements are representative of preventive and early intervention strategies.

Expand and Develop Appropriate Social Interactions

Build on social interactions between staff members and each student, including the student with challenging behaviors. Demonstrating positive regard for the student beyond the current behavior will help the child to feel a part of the group. Give additional attention when the student shows interest in a topic or attempts to engage staff appropriately. When the student goes off-task, steer the child toward more appropriate activities through redirection. Do not feed into inappropriate attention seeking by overreacting to disruptive behaviors; such behaviors are probably reinforced by adult interest, negativity, and concern.

Facilitate Appropriate Peer Interaction

Use group activities to build positive social interaction among students. Teach appropriate social language, how to interact reciprocally, and strategies for getting attention from others and for getting needs met. Teach appropriate language for social interactions during board games, recess activities, snack time, or group discussions. Provide opportunities for cooperative learning.

Review and Rehearse Daily Schedule

Students with significant memory impairments, some learning disabilities, emotional disturbances, autism, or mental retardation are frequently anxious during change or transition. They adapt very well to consistent scheduling and routine. Eventually, they learn most of the routines and can be very resistant to change. This internalization of routine is a means of control, and a student can become quite agitated, act silly, or be disruptive when experiencing unexpected change.

One means for compensating for this problem and building in functional academic experience is verbal rehearsal of scheduling. At the start of the day, go over the sequence of classroom activities verbally and pictorially, if possible. The pictures, icons, logos, and line drawings should be kept with the student for continuous reference. Sequence, not time, should be the emphasis of these rehearsals, but as an incidental training activity, the time of a particular activity also could be displayed beside it. This technique is a concrete and functional approach to reading and time-telling. In addition, it helps to relieve any anxiety associated with change and transition within a hectic or busy environment. This schedule can become a crutch when adult attention at transition time is not available, and it can be used in preparing the student for change on any given day. Knowing how long they have to wait for playtime or free time is important for many students. Coordinate the use of the schedule with other staff members working with the student so that information on the schedule will be accurate. Do not schedule and rehearse events that cannot be delivered reliably. The schedules can allow the student greater awareness, but if not followed consistently, they will irritate rather than reassure the student.

Review and Rehearse Classroom Rules

Actively teach easily generalized, specific rules. Rule teaching is a primary strategy for students with difficulties in concept formation and generalization. Rules should be stated as positive behaviors, such as "hands and feet to self" rather than "no hitting." They may have to be shown to the student in a very concrete fashion, and they may need to be stated before the student begins work. For example, before beginning the lesson, the teacher might show the student a picture of the student or a classmate working appropriately. The teacher would state, "The rule is you must work quietly." The student would then be asked to repeat the rule, and the student would be reinforced for following that rule.

Initially, only one to two rules should be taught at a time. It is important that the student internalize each rule in turn before others are taught contingently. The student may not always succeed in observing the rule, but the teacher must be consistent in expectations. Reminders of the rule should be given whenever the student does not follow it. Initially, all work should be evaluated by the student's ability to follow the rules while working. Quality and quantity of work are not the issue at this time. As the student acquires rules-driven classroom behavior and exhibits an interest in school work, quality and quantity can be re-evaluated. Also, rehearse appropriate rules and strategies before activities begin that may be difficult for the student.

Use Schedules Within Activities to Enhance Structures

It is equally important to structure tasks clearly and concretely when asking the student to work independently. Making the student aware of behavioral expectations, task sequence, and duration may be necessary to support focusing on the activity without distraction, undue anxiety, or disruptive and demanding behavior. The use of written or pictorial schedules may be of use here. Schedules can be used situationally to show the order of events within an activity, as in this example:

1. Use your name stamp on this paper.

2. Circle what you need for this activity.

3. Hand in your work.

Pictures or line drawings are available through many educational resources, especially through speech and language service providers or in critical/functional skills curricula. If the student can read, then short, simple sentences will suffice, along with pictures to enhance communication when possible and desirable.

Teach Coping Skills

This strategy can be especially effective when students are having difficulty following rules. Teach rules in motivating settings and during motivating activities. When a student is involved in motivating activities, remind him or her of the rules for appropriate behavior. Have the student occasionally state the rule when in danger of not following it. When the student is not involved in motivating activities or when activities become too stimulating or anxiety producing, teach the student to state a need to escape; for example, "It's too hard!" or "I need to leave!" or "I need help!" Any verbal explanation that allows the student to escape in an appropriate manner will do. When the student is aware of appropriate options for escaping difficult tasks or for reducing sensory stimuli, then it will be possible to negotiate with a rule, such as, "Try your best!" If the student is agitated or upset, teaching the child to use a relaxation area, such as a corner with a mat or pillows, may be a helpful additional coping strategy if consistently used.

Focus on Whole-Class Positive Behavior

Use the end of the class to comment on positive achievement of all class members. Allow all students to comment on good things they saw others doing. Build a classroom spirit around following classroom rules. Use stickers, praise, applause, additional playtime, or edibles as appropriate when doing this group activity.

Select and Teach Replacement Behaviors

1. *What are replacement behaviors?* In addition to manipulating the environment and integrating whole-classroom positive strategies, a positive approach to behavioral intervention teaches students replacement behaviors that will be as effective in meeting their needs as their challenging behaviors have been. Here are some examples:

- Allison learns to ask for a hug from her teachers and peers instead of roughhousing with them whenever she needs attention.
- Joseph learns to take a pass from the teacher's desk and go visit another adult (principal, nurse, janitor) whenever he

feels anxious. The pass is signed by his teacher and the other supportive adult to ensure accountability.

- Malcolm learns to ask for help from a peer partner when he feels he can't do a problem, instead of swearing or shouting.

2. *Guidelines for selecting replacement behaviors.* Replacement behaviors should always be selected with student, family, and educator input and practiced with all people involved. Students engage in challenging behaviors to meet specific needs. When selecting replacement behaviors, the team should address the following questions. Will the replacement behavior

- work as well as the challenging behavior in meeting the student's needs?
- be an acceptable alternative to the challenging behavior?
- be something that the student chooses to do and that is supported by family and teachers?
- help build a positive reputation for the student?

A replacement behavior can be a new behavior or a behavior the student already performs but not on a regular basis. For example, Allison knows how to ask for a hug, but she does not ask for one consistently. By encouraging and rewarding Allison to ask for a hug, Allison's teachers are able to teach an acceptable alternative to hitting. Joseph, on the other hand, is introduced to a new way of coping: he is taught to pick up a pass from the teacher's desk and leave the room when he feels anxious.

3. *Strategies for teaching replacement behavior.* There are a number of strategies for teaching replacement behavior. Once the team chooses a replacement behavior, consider the following tips and ideas for teaching it:

- Identify what the student has learned during the past year and find out what teaching strategies and assistance were most effective.
- In the beginning, practice the new behavior when the student is calm and relaxed and when problems are not occurring.
- Provide multiple opportunities for the student to role-play and practice using the new behavior (e.g., in different classes, recess, home).
- In addition to teaching the student *how* to perform the new behavior, teach *when* to use it.
- To teach the student to self-initiate performing the skill, use such procedures as role-playing and practice with feedback

in the natural environment. Teach the student to recognize the specific situational and internal cues (e.g., the student's heart is pounding just before it is time to read aloud) that naturally happen before the behavior should occur. Overall, minimize the use of teacher-related cues because they foster dependency on the teacher.

- Try to anticipate when the student is about to make a mistake (experience difficulty when initially learning a new coping skill) and provide support to ensure success, but make sure to allow enough time for the student to self-initiate participation. Ask what the student wants you to *do* (nonverbal cues) or *say* (verbal cues) to cue him or her to practice the new skill.

- Recognize that we all need different levels of support at different times. Be willing to increase or decrease the level of support based on the moment-to-moment needs of the student.

References

Chapter 3

Adolphs, R., Tranel, D., & Denburg, N. (2000). Impaired emotional declarative memory following unilateral amygdala damage. *Learning and Memory, 7*, 180–186.

Agosta, E., Graetz, J. E., Mastropieri, M. A., & Scruggs, T. E. (2004). Teacher-researcher partnerships to improve social behavior through social stories. *Intervention in School and Clinic, 39*, 276–287.

Anderson, A. K., & Phelps, E. A. (2002). Is the human amygdala critical for the subjective experience of emotion? Evidence of intact dispositional affect in patients with amygdala lesions. *Journal of Cognitive Neuroscience, 14*, 709–720.

Aron, A. R., Behrens, T. E., Smith, S., Frank, M. J., & Poldrack, R. A. (2007, April). Triangulating a cognitive control network using diffusion-weighted magnetic resonance imaging (MRI) and functional MRI. *Journal of Neuroscience, 27*, 3743–3752.

Battin-Pearson, S., Newcomb, M. D., Abbott, R. D., Hill, K. G., Catalano, R. F., & Hawkins, J. (2000). Predictors of early high school dropout: A test of five theories. *Journal of Educational Psychology, 92*, 586–582.

Botvin, G. J., & Griffin, K. W. (2004). Life skills training: Empirical findings and future directions. *Journal of Primary Prevention, 25*, 211–232.

Damasio, A. (2003). *Looking for Spinoza: Joy, sorrow, and the feeling brain.* New York: Harcourt.

Damasio, A. R., Grabowski, T. J., Bechara, A., Damasio, H., Ponto, L. L., Parvizi, J., & Hichwa, R. D. (2000). Subcortical and cortical brain activity during the feeling of self-generated emotions. *Nature Neuroscience, 3*, 1049–1056.

Ellickson, P. L., McCaffrey, D. F., Ghosh-Dastidar, B., & Longshore, D. L. (2003). New inroads in preventing adolescent drug use: Results from a large-scale trial of Project ALERT in middle schools. *American Journal of Public Health, 93*, 1830–1836.

Fleming, C. B., Haggerty, K. P., Catalano, R. F., Harachi, T. W., Mazza, J. J., & Gruman, D. H. (2005, November). Do social and behavioral characteristics targeted by preventive interventions predict standardized test scores and grades? *Journal of School Health, 75*, 342–349.

Gazzaniga, M. S., Ivry, R. B., & Mangun, G. R. (2002). *Cognitive neuroscience: The biology of the mind.* New York: Norton.

Haggerty, N. K., Black, R. S., & Smith, G. J. (2005). Increasing self-managed coping skills through social stories and apron storytelling. *Teaching Exceptional Children, 37*, 40–47.

Hart, A. J., Whalen, P. J., Shin, L. M., McInerney, S. C., Fischer, H., & Rausch, S. L. (2000). Differential response in the human amygdala to racial outgroup vs. ingroup face stimuli. *NeuroReport, 11*, 2351–2355.

Jaime, K., & Knowlton, E. (2007). Visual supports for students with behavior and cognitive challenges. *Intervention in School and Clinic, 42,* 259–270.

Johnstone, T., van Reekum, C. M., Oakes, T. R., & Davidson, R. J. (2006). The voice of emotion: an fMRI study of neural responses to angry and happy vocal expressions. *Social, Cognitive, & Affective Neuroscience, 1,* 242–249.

Kurzban, R., Tooby, J., & Cosmides, L. (2001). Can race be erased? Coalitional computation and social categorization. *Proceedings of the National Academy of Sciences, 98*(26), 15387–15392.

Lane, K. L., Givner, C. C., & Pierson, M. R. (2004). Teacher expectations of student behavior: Social skills necessary for success in elementary school classrooms. *Journal of Special Education, 38,* 104–110.

MacLean, P. D. (1952). Some psychiatric implications of physiological studies on frontotemporal portion of limbic system (visceral brain). *Electroencephalography and Clinical Neurophysiology, 4,* 407–418.

Massachusetts General Hospital (MGH) (2006). *Interventions in School.* Available online at www.school psychiatry.org.

McNeal, R. B., Jr., Hansen, W. B., Harrington, N. G., & Giles, S. M. (2004, April). How All Stars works: an examination of program effects on mediating variables. *Health Education and Behavior, 31,* 165–178.

Newcomb, M. D., Abbott, R. D., Catalano, R. F., Hawkins, J., Battin, S. R., & Hill, K. G. (2002). Mediational and deviance theories of late high school failure: Process roles of structural strains, academic competence, and general versus specific problem behavior. *Journal of Counseling Psychology, 49,* 172–186.

Ochsner, K., & Lieberman, M. (2001). The emergence of social cognitive neuroscience. *American Psychologist, 56,* 717–734.

Parsons, L. D. (2006). Using video to teach social skills to secondary students with autism. *Teaching Exceptional Children, 39,* 32–39.

Paus, T. (2005). Mapping brain maturation and cognitive development during adolescence. *Trends in Cognitive Sciences, 9,* 60–68.

Phelps, E. A., O'Connor, K. J., Cunningham, W. A., Funayama, E. S., Gatenby, J. C., Gore, J. C., & Banaji, M. R. (2000). Performance on indirect measures of race evaluation predicts amygdala activation. *Journal of Cognitive Neuroscience, 12,* 729–738.

Phelps, E. A., & Thomas, L. A. (2003). Race, behavior, and the brain: The role of neuroimaging in understanding complex social behaviors. *Political Psychology, 24,* 747–758.

Redenbach, S. (2004). *Self-esteem and emotional intelligence: The necessary ingredients for success.* Davis, CA: ESP Wise Publications.

Restak, R. (2000). *Mysteries of the mind.* Washington, DC: National Geographic Society.

Rogers, M. F., & Myles, B. S. (2001). Using social stories and comic strip conversations to interpret social situations for an adolescent with Asperger syndrome. *Intervention In School and Clinic, 36,* 310–313.

Rolls, E. T. (1999). *The brain and emotion.* Oxford, UK: Oxford University Press.

Schneier, F. R. (2003, September). Social anxiety disorder: Is common, underdiagnosed, impairing, and treatable. *British Medical Journal, 327,* 515–516.

Steinberg, L. (2005, February). Cognitive and affective development in adolescence. *Trends in Cognitive Sciences, 9,* 69–74.

Stipek, D. (2006, September). Relationships matter. *Educational Leadership, 64,* 46–49.

Chapter 4

Albert, L. (1989). *A teacher's guide to cooperative discipline: How to manage your classroom and promote self-esteem*. Circle Pines, MN: American Guidance Service.

Barr, R. D., & Parrett, W. H. (2003). *Saving our students: Saving our schools: 50 proven strategies for revitalizing at-risk students and low-performing schools*. Thousand Oaks, CA: Corwin.

Bellanca, J., & Fogarty, R. (2003). *Blueprint for achievement in the cooperative classroom* (3rd ed.). Thousand Oaks, CA: Corwin.

Burke, K. (2006). *From standards to rubrics in six steps: Tools for assessing student learning, K–8*. Thousand Oaks, CA: Corwin.

Burke, K. (2005). *How to assess authentic learning* (4th ed.).Thousand Oaks, CA: Corwin.

Curwin, R. L., & Mendler, A. N. (1988). *Discipline with dignity*. Alexandria, VA: Association for Supervision and Curriculum Development.

DeRoche, E. F., & Williams, M. M. (2001). *Character education: A primer for teachers*. Allen, TX: Argus Communications.

Dinkmeyer, D., & Losoncy, L. E. (1980). *The encouragement book. Becoming a positive person*. New York: Prentice-Hall.

Dinkmeyer, D., McKay, G. D., & Dinkmeyer, D., Jr. (1980). *Systematic training for effective teaching*. Circle Pines, MN: American Guidance Service.

Gholar, C. R., & Riggs, E. G. (2004). *Connecting with students' will to succeed: The power of conation*. Thousand Oaks, CA: Corwin.

Given, B. K. (2002). *Teaching to the brain's natural learning systems*. Alexandria, VA: Association for Supervision and Curriculum Development.

Glasser, W. (1986). *Control theory in the classroom*. New York: Harper & Row.

Gough, P. B. (1987). The key to improving schools: An interview with William Glasser. *Phi Delta Kappan, 68*(9), 656–662.

Holland, H. (2007). Can educators close the achievement gap? An interview with Richard Rothstein and Kati Haycock. *The Journal of Staff Development, 28*(1), 54–62.

Jones, V. F., & Jones, L. S. (1998). *Comprehensive classroom management: Creating communities of support and solving problems* (5th ed.). Boston: Allyn & Bacon.

Kauffman, J. M., Hallahan, D. P., Mostert, M. P., Trent, S. C., & Nuttycombe, D. G. (1993). *Managing classroom behavior: A reflective case-based approach*. Needham Heights, MA: Allyn & Bacon.

Levin, J., & Nolan, J. F. (1996). *Principles of classroom management: A professional decision-making model* (2nd ed.). Boston: Allyn & Bacon.

Mendler, A. N. (1997). *Power struggles: Successful techniques for educators*. Rochester, NY: Discipline Associates.

Roberts, W. B., Jr. (2006). *Bullying from both sides: Strategic interventions for working with bullies and victims*. Thousand Oaks, CA: Corwin.

Shore, K. (2005). *The ABCs of bully prevention: A comprehensive schoolwide approach*. Port Chester, NY: DUDE Publishing.

Short, P. M., Short, R. J., & Blanton, C. (1994). *Rethinking student discipline: Alternatives that work*. Thousand Oaks, CA: Corwin.

Tileston, D. W. (2004). *What every teacher should know about classroom management and discipline*. Thousand Oaks, CA: Corwin.

Vaughn, S., Bos, C. S., & Schumm, J. S. (2000). *Teaching exceptional, diverse and at-risk students in the general education classroom* (2nd ed.). Boston: Allyn & Bacon.

Weiner, L. (1999). *Urban teaching: The essentials*. New York: Teachers College Press.

Wolfgang, C. H., Bennett, B. J., & Irvin, J. L. (1999). *Strategies for teaching self-discipline in the middle grades*. Boston: Allyn & Bacon.

Chapter 5

Burke, K. (1992). *What to do with the kid who: Developing cooperation, self-discipline, and responsibility in the classroom*. Palatine, IL: IRI Skylight.

Given, B. (2002). *Teaching to the brain's natural learning systems*. Alexandria, VA: Association for Supervision and Curriculum Development.

Glasser, W. (1986). *Control theory in the classroom*. New York: Harper and Row.

Jones, F. (2002). Available online at www.fredjones.com

Linnoila, M., Virkkunen, M., Scheinin, M., Nuutila, A., Rimon, R., & Goodwin, F. K. (1994). Low cerebrospinal fluid 5-hydroxyindoleacetic acid concentration differentiates impulse from nonimpulsive violent behavior. In R. Masters & M. McGuire (Eds.), *The neurotransmitter revolution: Serotonin, social behavior, and the law* (pp. 62–68). Carbondale: Southern Illinois University Press.

Master Teacher. (2002). Available online at www.disciplinehelp.com.

Panksepp, J. (1998). *Affective neuroscience: The foundations of human and animal emotions*. New York: Oxford University Press.

Payne, R. K. (2001). *A framework for understanding poverty*. Highlands, TX: Aha! Process Inc.

Chapter 6

Glasser, W. (1990). *Reality therapy*. New York: HarperCollins.

Horner, R. H., Sugai, G., Todd, A. W., & Lewis-Palmer, T. (2005). School-wide positive behavior support: An alternative approach to discipline in schools. In L. Bambara & L. Kern (Eds.), *Individualized supports for students with problem behaviors: Designing positive behavior plans* (pp. 359–390). New York: Guilford Press.

Sugai, G. (2000). Instituting school-wide behavior supports. *CEC Today, 6*(7), 5.

Sugai, G., & Horner, R. H. (2002). The evolution of discipline practices: School-wide positive behavior supports. *Child and Family Behavior Therapy, 24*, 23–50.

Sugai, G., Sprague, J. R., Horner, R. H., & Walker, H. M. (2000). Preventing school violence: The use of office discipline referrals to assess and monitor school-wide discipline interventions. *Journal of Emotional and Behavioral Disorders, 8*(2), 94–101.

Chapter 7

DiGiuseppe, R., & Tafrate, R. C. (2007). *Understanding anger disorders*. New York: Oxford University Press.

Kohn, A. (1998). *What to look for in a classroom . . . and other essays*. San Francisco: Jossey-Bass.

Lochman, J., Dunn, S. E., & Klimes-Dougan, B. (1993). An intervention and consultation model from a social cognitive perspective: A description of the anger coping program. *School Psychology Review, 22*(3), 458–471.

Noteboom, J. T., Barnholt, K. R., & Enoka, R. M. (2001). Activation of the arousal response and impairment of performance increase with anxiety and stressor intensity. *Journal of Applied Physiology, 91*, 2093–2101.

Oldfather, P. (1993). What students say about motivating experiences in a whole language classroom. *The Reading Teacher, 46*(8), 672–681.

Oldfather, P., & Thomas, S. (1999). The nature and outcomes of students' longitudinal participatory research on literacy motivations and schooling. *Research in the Teaching of English, 34*, 281–320.

Perry, B. D. (2006). *The boy who was raised as a dog and other stories from a child psychiatrist's notebook: What traumatized children can teach us about loss, love, and healing.* New York: Basic Books.

Polowy, M. (1992, April). *Effective management of angry, hostile, aggressive children.* Paper presented at the eighth annual training symposium of the Georgia Council on Child Abuse, Atlanta.

Prothrow-Stith, D., & Weissman, M. (1993). *Deadly consequences: How violence is destroying our teenage population and a plan to begin solving the problem.* New York: Harper & Row.

Rachman, S. (1979). *The concept of required helpfulness. Behavior, Research, and Therapy,* 17(1), 1–6.

Tice, D., & Baumeister, R. (1993). Controlling anger: Self-induced emotion change. In D. M. Wegner & J. W. Pennebaker (Eds.), *Handbook of mental control* (pp. 393–410). Englewood Cliffs, NJ: Prentice Hall.

Werner, E. E., & Smith, R. S. (2001). *Journeys from childhood to midlife.* Ithaca, NY: Cornell University Press.

Zillman, D. (1993). Mental control of angry aggression. In D. M. Wegner & J. W. Pennebaker (Eds.), *Handbook of mental control* (pp. 370–393). Englewood Cliffs, NJ: Prentice Hall.

Zimrin, H. (1986). A profile of survival. *Child Abuse and Neglect, 10,* 339–349.

Chapter 8

Adler, J., & Springen, K. (1999, May 3). How to fight back. *Newsweek.* Available from www.newsweek.com/id/88189

Bluestein, J. (2001). *Creating emotionally safe schools.* Deerfield Beach, FL: Health Communications.

Bluestein, J. (2008). *The win-win classroom.* Thousand Oaks, CA: Corwin.

Bluestein, J., & Katz, E. (2005). *High school's not forever.* Deerfield Beach, FL: Health Communications.

Blum, R. W., McNeely, C., & Rinehart, P. M. (2002). *Improving the odds: The untapped power of schools to improve the health of teens.* Minneapolis: University of Minnesota, Center for Adolescent Health and Development.

Blumenfeld, B. (1996, October 2). Moral education not rote learning [Letter to the editor]. *Albuquerque Journal,* p. A11.

Cichy, B. (2008, February). *Functional behavior assessment on-the-fly.* Paper presented at Minnesota Council for Exceptional Children conference, Duluth, MN.

Freiberg, J. A. (2007c). *Improving school climate to diminish bullying behaviors: Creating "climates of respect"* [PowerPoint slides].

Gatto, J. T. (2005). *Dumbing us down: The hidden curriculum of compulsory schooling.* Gabriola Island, British Columbia, Canada: New Society.

Gazzaniga, M. S. (1988). *Mind matters.* Boston: Houghton Mifflin.

Haslam, S. (2001, September). *Emotions are a fact of life* [Conference handout].

Isaacson, W. (2007). *Einstein.* New York: Simon & Schuster.

Kenmore, C. (n.d.). In *Motivation quotes.* Available from www.famousquotesand authors.com/authors/carolyn_kenmore_quotes.html

Littke, D., & Grabelle, S. (2004). *The big picture: Education is everyone's business.* Alexandria, VA: Association for Supervision and Curriculum Development.

Mahoney, A. S., & Purr, C. (2007). *Untenured, uncensored.* Lanham, MD: Rowman & Littlefield.

Mann, H. (n.d.). In *Famous quotes and authors: Punishments quotes.* Available from www.famous quotesandauthors.com/topics/punishment_quotes.html

Marshall, M. (n.d.). *The social development program: Ensuring social responsibility* [Conference handout].

Marshall, M. (2001). *Discipline without stress, punishments, or rewards: How teachers and parents promote responsibility and learning.* Los Alamitos, CA: Piper Press.

National Education Association. (1975). *Code of ethics.* Retrieved from www.nea.org/home/30442.htm

Naylor, A. (2009a, February 28). *3 Keys to personal accountability and creating a better life.* Available from www.huffingtonpost.com/anne-naylor/3-keys-to-personal-accoun_b_169736.html

Naylor, A. (2009b, February 14). *5 ways to turn on the power of your love.* Available from www.huffingtonpost.com/anne-naylor/5-ways-to-turn-on-the-pow_b_166619.html

NYCLU, Annenberg Institute release report on successful and safe NYC schools that say no to aggressive police tactics. (2009). Available from www.nyclu.org/node/2501

Osborn, D. K., & Osborn, J. D. (1977). *Discipline and classroom management.* Athens, GA: Education Associates.

Purkey, W. W., & Aspy, D. N. (1988, February). The mental health of students: Nobody minds? Nobody cares? *Person-Centered Review, 3*(1), 41–49.

Quimby, D. (2003, May). Overworked and under-appreciated: A tribute to teachers. *Teachers.net Gazette.* Available from http://teachers.net/gazette/MAY03/quimby.html

Reynolds, M. R., & Reynolds, C. (2008). *The power of connection* [Video file]. Available from www.connectionmovie.com/

School violence: The history of school discipline. (1998). Available from http://law.jrank.org/pages/12094/School-Violence-history-school-discipline.html

Underwood, A. (2005, October 3). *The good heart. Newsweek,* 49–55.

Wyatt, R. L., & White, J. E. (2007). *Making your first year a success* (2nd ed.). Thousand Oaks, CA: Corwin.

Zimmerman, J. (2007, July 1). Justice Thomas got it wrong: Goal of schools isn't discipline. *St. Paul Pioneer Press.*

Chapter 9

Boeckmann, D., Cardelli, G., & Jacobs, J. (1989). *Alternatives for persons who are behaviorally challenged.* Crystal, MN: Hennepin Technical College, District #287.

Pierangelo, R. (2004). *The special educator's survival guide* (2nd ed.). San Francisco: Jossey-Bass.

Pierangelo, R., & Giuliani, G. (2006). *Assessment in special education: A practical approach* (2nd ed.). Boston: Allyn and Bacon.

Topper, K., Williams, W., Leo, K., Hamilton, R., & Fox, T. (1994, January). *A positive approach to understanding and addressing challenging behaviors: Supporting educators and families to include students with emotional and behavioral difficulties in regular education.* Burlington: University of Vermont, Center on Disability and Community Inclusion.

CORWIN
A SAGE Company

The Corwin logo—a raven striding across an open book—represents the union of courage and learning. Corwin is committed to improving education for all learners by publishing books and other professional development resources for those serving the field of PreK–12 education. By providing practical, hands-on materials, Corwin continues to carry out the promise of its motto: **"Helping Educators Do Their Work Better."**